What people are saying about …

Fearless Families

"Another excellent writing by Kevin Thompson. This is a must-read for all families no matter their uniqueness. The family has been at the tip of the spear in the present days of uncertainty, making this a timely source for a new path for our families. With much fear in the world today, this is an easy read with practical yet thoughtful paradigm shifts that will impact how you see and lead your family from the inner circle to the outside relationships."

Marty Sloan, lead pastor of Calvary
Church, Naperville, IL

"With so much going on in the world today, it is easy to feel hopeless and fearful; however, we must remember that fear is not a characteristic of our God. Kevin has outlined and given tangible ways to acknowledge and make a choice to choose the Father's perfect love that casts out all fear!"

Gus and Kristi Malzahn, former
head football coach at Auburn University

"Fearless Families is an excellent resource not just for families but for leaders and people at all ages and stages of life. In the midst of the fear and uncertainty of today's world, Kevin Thompson brings

a powerful and practical word of courage and hope. I strongly encourage you to read this book and apply its principles!"

Dr. Danny Wood, senior pastor of
Shades Mountain Baptist Church

"Being a coach for forty-two years, I can say without hesitation how important this book will be to parents, coaches, and teachers. Teachers and coaches see the aftermath, every single day, of families being ruled by fear. When you read the headlines or watch the news, it is difficult not to withdraw into the 'house of fear.' This book is important and relevant because it doesn't take the easy route by just explaining or complaining about the problem. It offers a roadmap to guide and direct a family or a team through the challenging times before us. Don't just read it, WORK it."

Rick Jones, senior assistant to head
coach at University of Missouri, 2012
National Federation of High Schools
National Football Coach of the Year

"With relatable examples and clear prose, Kevin Thompson gets to the heart of what motivates fear and reminds us how the gospel gives us the hope we need to live unafraid. This practical guide will challenge and encourage you."

Dr. O. Alan Noble, associate professor of
English and author of *Disruptive Witness:*
Speaking Truth in a Distracted Age

"Kevin Thompson has insightfully written about the needs of families in a time when we need tremendous guidance. Readers will appreciate how real the book is when discussing the family issues that plague so many of us, including the anxiety of parents, relating to in-laws, and the love needed to overcome the stress of family life today. Fathers and mothers will greatly profit from reading this accessible book as Kevin discusses the 'Home of the Afraid.' He places his finger on the pulse of our American culture when he writes of our idol of safety and the deceptive lies we have convinced ourselves of. Throughout this timely book, Kevin relates solid biblical thinking to the needs of parents and children. I encourage you to read this book and apply the principles to your home."

Scott Maze, PhD, pastor of North Richland Hills Baptist Church

FEARLESS

FAMILIES

FEARLESS
FAMILIES

Building Brave Homes
in an Uncertain World

KEVIN A. THOMPSON

DAVID C COOK

transforming lives together

FEARLESS FAMILIES
Published by David C Cook
4050 Lee Vance Drive
Colorado Springs, CO 80918 U.S.A.

Integrity Music Limited, a Division of David C Cook
Brighton, East Sussex BN1 2RE, England

The graphic circle C logo is a registered trademark of David C Cook.

Library of Congress Control Number 2020946263
ISBN 978-0-8307-8135-5
eISBN 978-0-8307-8136-2

The Team: Michael Covington, David Webb, James Hershberger,
Megan Stengel, Jack Campbell, Susan Murdock
Cover Design: Jon Middel
Cover Image: Getty Images

Printed in the United States of America
First Edition 2021

1 2 3 4 5 6 7 8 9 10

121620

To Silas, your courage inspired this book.
To Ella, your love empowers others.
To Jenny, you woo me beyond where I'm
comfortable and into a far greater adventure.

Contents

Introduction

Diagnosis: Fear

You will not fear the terror of night, nor the arrow
that flies by day, nor the pestilence that stalks in the
darkness, nor the plague that destroys at midday.

Psalm 91:5–6 NIV

The school bell would ring in five minutes. In any other house, still being at home this close to the opening bell might cause a state of alarm. For us, however, living two blocks from the school meant this was a typical Wednesday morning. For the past five years, our routine had been the same. At 7:55 a.m., the kids would meet me at the front door, and I would walk them to school.

A year earlier, things had changed for my son. Although we held hands walking down the block and across the street, the moment we stepped onto school property, Silas let go of my hand and walked a few steps in front of me. "It's okay, Daddy," my daughter said quietly, still holding my hand, "he's just trying to be somebody."

Aren't we all? I thought.

As my nine-year-old son ran on ahead each day, my twelve-year-old daughter continued to walk with me. Having a child with special needs creates a different set of concerns for a parent. While Down syndrome didn't prevent Ella from being able to walk into her classroom alone, it comforted me to see the setting in which she would spend her day, to look her teacher in the eye and have that teacher see me.

One morning, Ella met me at the back door as usual, but Silas was nowhere in sight. I figured he was grabbing his lunch or still putting on his shoes. I called out, "Time to go!" but heard nothing in reply. "Stay here," I said to my daughter and went to search for her brother. He wasn't in the kitchen, the living room, or his bedroom. I finally found him in a little nook by the front door. He appeared to be panicked and a little ashamed.

A year later, my wife, Jenny, and I sat in a psychologist's office and heard the words "school refusal" for the first time. School refusal is a recognized disorder in which a child refuses to go to school on a regular basis or has problems staying in school, often due to fear or anxiety. It explained so much. Silas was often unable to sleep on school nights. The horrible acid reflux that had plagued him since second grade was mostly absent during the summer. Then there was the recurring vomiting, which only took place on Sunday evenings.

We now had a better idea as to the nature of the problem, but a diagnosis doesn't change things. "School refusal" described Silas's situation but didn't solve it. It gave us some insights but not a game plan. What were we supposed to do with a straight-A student who wasn't struggling academically or socially? He wasn't being bullied. He wasn't isolated. From the outside looking in, everything seemed to be great. But inside he was struggling, and that struggle expressed itself in dramatic ways to do whatever it took to avoid his greatest fear.

Jenny and I aren't high-stress people by nature, although we are busy. Jenny owns a marketing company, and the work is demanding, requiring long hours. For me, pastoring a church means dealing with high expectations and watching over a lot of people. Yet we had created a laid-back home. Life was hard enough, and we had no interest in making it harder on ourselves or our children. Our marriage was good, and our parenting style was involved but relaxed. We intentionally refused many of the scheduling demands that stretch other families, often to the breaking point. We weren't perfect, but our home was a place we could go to rejuvenate before facing tomorrow's challenges.

But that all changed. Anxiety breeds anxiety, and as my son began to outwardly express what he was experiencing internally, we started changing our laid-back parenting style. We became anxious and fearful ourselves. Situations we previously would've navigated with a "He'll be fine" suddenly became "Let me go check" responses. Our son's emotional safety became paramount when making any decision. If he was nervous, we would find a different plan. Every option was evaluated according to how much stress it might cause. We became obsessed with protecting our son, not just emotionally but socially as well. We live in a small town, where rumors can spread quickly. And while we didn't want to lie to people, we did want to protect Silas, and so we tended to hide the appearance of any problems.

As time passed, we found ourselves avoiding difficult conversations with Ella and Silas, and the kids learned to manipulate us to take advantage of our fears and avoid disciplinary action. As for the school refusal problem, we would offer Silas big rewards for taking small steps, but everything felt like a perpetual power struggle with him. Nothing we did seemed to work. The more we tried to manage our son's anxiety, the more it simply added to our own.

High Time for a New Approach

After receiving the first report from the psychologist, I took it to my mother, a teacher whose career spanned four decades. I sat quietly as she read the evaluation. When she finished, she looked up and said, "Well, this explains so much … about you."

It was funny and true. While I never refused to attend school as a child, I had experienced many symptoms similar to my son's. Although the way I expressed stress had changed over the years, I once again found myself struggling with anxiety. Not only had our son inherited my predisposition toward anxiety, but he was now experiencing the consequences of my own anxious choices. Fear ruled us both, and it had begun to infect the rest of the family too. Every aspect of our home seemed to be directed by fear. We needed a different way.

The initial diagnosis came after months of testing; our plan to deal with it came in a moment of desperation. On an especially hard day, my wife firmly looked my son in the eye and said, "I know you're afraid right now, and that's okay. But we are not going to be ruled by fear. We are going to love you no matter what it feels like."

That was it. The plan was simple. Not easy, but simple. We would recognize fear and be compassionate and understanding with one another, but we would no longer make decisions based on our fears. Every choice would instead be a conscious decision made out of love. Where we were tempted to avoid tough conversations because of our anxieties, love would compel us to communicate honestly. Where our fear had often allowed our kids to manipulate us to avoid discipline, now love would drive us to set stronger boundaries and clarify consequences. Before, we were tempted to hide our family's problems in order to manage the opinions of others, but now love would enable us to ask for whatever help we needed, no matter who learned of our struggles.

It wasn't a magic formula, but it was the right paradigm. By choosing to identify and acknowledge fear but make decisions based on love, we discovered a way forward. This wasn't just a path for dealing with a child's anxiety; it was a healthy way to raise kids, tend to a marriage, and communicate as a family.

A Tale of Two Homes

This isn't a parenting book, although the lessons inside were discovered in the midst of a difficult season of parenting. It's not another marriage book, yet the concepts within may be more important to building a healthy marriage than the two marriage books I've written. It's not a book about leadership, business, or coaching, although I've shared these ideas with companies, leaders, and teams. The ideas in this book touch on all those issues, but at its core this is a story about two homes.

The first is a home ruled by fear. This home is never constructed on purpose or with vision but instead is cobbled together from instinct, intuition, ingrained patterns of self-destructive behavior, and odds and ends of pseudo-wisdom drawn from the culture we live in. No one would intentionally design a home this way, but nearly all of us end up in such a structure unless we have made some purposeful choices to do otherwise. I call this structure the Home of the Afraid. Here, fear rules the family (or company or team), and it leads us to trust in things that promise to quiet our fears yet never deliver on their promises.

The second home is defined by love. While fear is sometimes felt here, it's never allowed to become a dictator. Instead, the family (or company or team) makes the intentional choice to be guided by love in all of its actions and interactions. Love leads them to a different set of values and motivations—blueprints for a house that is sturdy, influential, and built to last. I call this the Home of the Brave, and it is a beautiful addition to any community.

Christ's command to "fear not" (Matthew 10:31) calls us to move out of the first home. His admonition to "love one another" (John 13:34) invites us to relocate and move into the second home.

Imagine what our lives—and the world—might be if we would simply live by these two directives.

Feel the Fear but Choose Love

What began as a realization that Jenny and I were making parenting decisions based on fear became an ongoing discovery of how fear is ruling every part of people's lives in today's world. On the one hand, our natural human response to that fear makes cognitive sense, but it rarely results in the outcome we desire. Rather than lessening our fears or helping us find comfort in times of stress, these responses increase our concerns. Only when we learn to feel fear without allowing ourselves to be ruled by it can we hope to arrive at a different, more satisfying outcome.

While our journey with my son led to this book, this isn't a book about his story. It's about our family's story. And your story. It's about how fear drives us to make wrong choices, leading us astray and tearing families—and therefore communities and nations—apart. My hope is that this book will reveal to you how love can transform your home and prepare your family to navigate a world of fear.

Part I

The Home of
the Afraid

Chapter 1

Fear Is a Bad Driver

Anxiety in a man's heart weighs him down.

Proverbs 12:25

*And which of you by being anxious can add a single hour
to his span of life? If then you are not able to do as small
a thing as that, why are you anxious about the rest?*

Luke 12:25–26

When I was in graduate school, I regularly went to lunch with a group of friends and a well-known professor. For many of us, Calvin Miller was the reason we had chosen this school, and he had taken us under his wing. Calvin was funny, generous, and oftentimes irreverent. Having achieved great popularity as a writer in the 1970s and '80s, by the early 2000s he was better known for inspiring author Max Lucado than for his own writings. But Calvin had been places, and it was fun to hear his insider's perspective on certain megachurches and the men and women behind them.

Yet as great as he was at preaching, teaching, and storytelling, Calvin was a horrible driver. Whenever he got behind the wheel with us in the car, we students would buckle up and rededicate ourselves to Jesus for fear that we might meet Him soon! The problem was that wherever Calvin looked, his hands followed. If there was a really nice car in the left lane, Calvin's eyes—and his car—would drift in that direction. If he had something to say to one of us in the back seat, rather than looking in the rearview mirror, he would turn around and talk to us as the car drifted to the right.

Finally, one day as we headed to lunch, I asked, "Calvin, do you mind if I drive?" He had no problem with my driving, but he was confused by the question. I told him, "Honestly, you're not a great driver. And if the four of us die in a car wreck today, next week's *Christianity Today* is going to read 'Calvin Miller and Three Others Dead,' and I would like a chance to make a name for myself before I die. I really don't want to be an 'other.'"

Some people are excellent drivers, and others are less so. Then there are the Calvin Millers of the world. Now, there's nothing immoral about having poor driving skills. And an inability to drive well doesn't mean a person shouldn't be allowed in a car. Even bad drivers have a right to enjoy the privileges of modern transportation. But poor drivers are far better suited to sitting in the back seat, where their shortcomings behind the wheel won't do damage to everyone else in the car.

Fear is a notoriously bad driver. While it's an acceptable, even expected, passenger, we should never allow fear to drive our decisions, attitudes, or perspectives. Yet the modern family is often ruled by fear.

Many of us parent primarily from a position of fear: *How do we raise them right? How do we avoid messing them up psychologically? How do we keep them reasonably happy, healthy, and responsible so they aren't still living with us in their forties?*

Marriages today are often driven by fear too. Many of us are afraid to reveal our true thoughts or say what is truly on our hearts. We long for more—more intimacy, more passion, more romance— but we don't do anything about it. And we turn a blind eye to obvious problems instead of confronting and solving them because we're afraid to have the difficult conversations.

Fear rarely leads to good decisions, yet so many of our choices, actions, and attitudes are based on the deep-seated fears residing within our hearts and minds. But it was never meant to be this way.

People were created from a place of perfect, infinite love—and we were intended to live in love for one another and to make choices each day based on that love. Yet love is expelled where fear is allowed to rule. Love fixates on meeting the needs of others, but fear focuses on fulfilling one's own needs and wants. We cannot truly love when we're afraid, because we cannot look beyond our own selfish desires to see to the well-being of the ones we're supposed to love.

Today's family is ruled by fear. It's a trait we inherited from the first family.

Living in the garden with a multitude of blessings, our original ancestors had only one restriction: don't eat of the fruit of the tree of knowledge. When the tempter slithered near Eve, he whispered that it was possible God was holding out on her. When Adam and Eve took the bait and ate the forbidden fruit, fear was born. God later found them hiding among the trees, and Adam said, "I heard the sound of you in the garden, and I was afraid, because I was naked, and I hid myself" (Genesis 3:10).

Fear greatly changed life for the first family. No longer were they free to live without worry, relate to each other without skepticism, or communicate to God without doubt. With one terrible decision, they exchanged complete peace for unending concern. Born in a moment of rebellion, fear would forever reside in the heart of every man, woman, and child.

Humanity now had a reason to be afraid.

Looking for Security in All the Wrong Places

As David observed, we are all but a step from death (1 Samuel 20:3). This wasn't the case before fear's birthday, but it's been an unavoidable reality ever since. Wars, diseases, accidents, natural disasters, the evil of others, our own foolish choices—all can have disastrous consequences for ourselves and those we love. Given the plethora of ways to die in this world, people have a right to be afraid.

Adam and Eve certainly had reasons to be frightened, as their lives were now in danger for the first time. For one thing, lions, tigers, and bears were suddenly no longer vegetarians. For another, as exiles from Eden, they faced an uncertain future in an inhospitable and unfamiliar world. But they also knew fear because the thing they had placed their trust in—the fruit—had failed them.

Fear is often caused by the failure of our idols.[1]

We all place our trust in something, and we have learned from our story-obsessed culture to design our lives around a personal narrative involving that trust:

If I love and/or pursue _____, I will
be safe (or successful or happy).

Whatever we fill in the blank with, we entrust that thing with our lives in exchange for our worship. We honor it. Give it time. Protect it. Value it. Organize our lives around it. All with the expectation that it will give us the life we want.

Our blanks are filled with a variety of things. Some people, like Eve, trust in knowledge. They believe that if they can simply accumulate and possess the right amount of information, they will be able to protect themselves from the ills of this world. Others put their trust in power, money, influence, fame, religion, a sports team, being a good person, and so on. Our options are limitless, but the outcomes are all the same.

No matter what we choose to fill in the blank, if it's not God with a capital *G*, that thing will not provide what it promises. It can't. Humanity is unable to create for itself a life free of fear and worry apart from God. Without divine intervention, fear is unavoidable. And when our idols fail us, the result is more fear. As King David wrote, we not only fear death and the unpleasant realities of life, but we also fear the failure of those things in which we place our trust. "The sorrows of those who run after another god shall multiply" (Psalm 16:4).

What will you do if your idols fail you?

What will you do if your emotional security is based on knowing that another person loves you, but then your spouse walks out on you?

What will you do if your identity is wrapped up in being seen as the perfect parent, but then your teenager is arrested for driving under the influence?

What will you do if your personal narrative says that as long as you're a good employee and faithful to your employer everything will be okay, but then your life is turned upside down when the economy takes a turn and your job is terminated?

What will you do if you've always believed that money and possessions will bring you peace, but even though you're living in a big house and driving a nice car, you're still having the same fights with your spouse and struggling with uncertainty?

When we place our trust in something other than God, and that thing fails us, the result is fear.

How Fear Expresses Itself

Fear is so prevalent in our lives that we have grown accustomed to it. We don't often think about air until we find ourselves struggling to breathe. We tend to forget it's there, and it's only when we stay too long underwater or linger in a smoke-filled room that air moves to the forefront of our thoughts. So unless you're confronted with immediate, life-threatening danger, how do you know when fear is present and affecting your choices?

In simpler times, it was easier to recognize the presence of fear. You're probably familiar with the term "fight-or-flight response." Recent work has identified "freeze" as a distinguishable third response option. When a threat was identified outside their camp, our ancestors basically had three choices: fight, flee, or freeze. If an army was approaching or an animal was about to attack, they could react by (1) standing their ground and fighting, (2) running from the threat, or (3) freezing, whether paralyzed by fear or in hopes the threat would not see them and simply pass by.

Today, if someone breaks into your home, fight, flight, and freeze are still your primary options. They can be perfectly viable responses when your life is in danger or you feel physically threatened.

But what about when you feel *emotionally* threatened?

Your wife says, "We need to talk."

Your teenager comes in after curfew.

Your toddler won't stay in his or her bed.

These are not scenarios in which fight, flight, and freeze are appropriate responses. Yes, these situations all require effort and energy to determine the proper course of action, but they should not pose such an immediate threat to our well-being that we respond with fear. But how often do we do just that?

When our heart rates rise, our tones stiffen, our voices raise, and our muscles tighten, we need to determine just what it is we're afraid of. There are times when we have reasons to be afraid, but we should not live in a constant state of fear. Our homes should not be defined by fear. Try as we might to protect our loved ones from outside threats, families should never fear one another. Instead, our interactions and the climate of our homes should be defined by love. Fight, flight, and freeze have little place in our most important relationships. Yet so often we fall back on these instinctive reactions in moments of stress. Consider the following.

Fight

Rather than engaging in a productive conversation about an important issue, your teen responds in a knee-jerk fashion to something you've said, and the interaction quickly devolves into an all-out fight. Social media might be the most visible example of how much fear dominates communication in our culture. Facebook fights and Twitter wars are by-products of fear.

Interactions between generations can be contentious for a variety of reasons, but fear is the greatest driver of these conflicts. Both parties are terrified of change, their current uncertainty, and what the future might hold. Full of fear, they fight.

Flight

She can tell something is wrong. She asks how you are doing, and you tersely respond, "Fine." Whether the other person is your spouse, boss, coworker, or friend, you're hiding your true feelings from that person, and hiding is a form of flight. You don't want to engage the issue at hand, so you deny it by "running."

There is a right time to flee, but far more often we use flight as a way to avoid talking with others or confronting our own emotions. We flee circumstances, relationships, accountability, and tensions. So often, when we should fully engage with a situation, we run instead. We do so because we are afraid.

Freeze

You're at the barbershop. All five chairs are filled by customers getting their hair cut, and others are waiting for their turns. Several of the barbers and their customers are conversing about border security. There are differing opinions, and the discussion is good and respectful. Then an older man says loudly, "All those illegals are just murderers and rapists!"

The man's statement has no statistical basis in fact, and it doesn't reflect the character of the undocumented people you interact with on a daily basis. The statement comes from a place of ignorance and bigotry, yet no one refutes it. Afraid of increasing tension, of being considered un-American, or of being singled out, no one says anything. Because of fear, everyone freezes in the hope that someone changes the subject.

Fight, flight, and freeze characterize our actions far more than we realize. While these responses can protect us when real danger is present, they damage us and our relationships when we wrongly use them to respond to people out of fear. The instinct that protects us from danger becomes a danger itself when wrongly applied. Family and home were made for love, not fear.

Love doesn't respond to such situations with fight, flight, or freeze. Love responds with courageous personal connection and vulnerability. Instead of fighting, love peacefully listens or lets another person have a differing opinion or engages in a meaningful conversation. Instead of fleeing, love causes us to move toward people, embrace the tension, and actively attempt to serve them. Instead of freezing, love drives us to take action. It calls us out of our comfort zones—out of ourselves—and into significant engagement.

Fight, flight, or freeze was useful when our ancestors lived on the prairie and predators stalked the horizon, looking for the right moment to attack. But they are horrible responses in the modern home. Fight, flight, or freeze might save you from a grizzly bear, but they will kill any hope you have for intimacy and growth you might experience with your spouse and children.

The Faulty Design of the Modern Home

Whether we recognize it or not, fear often rules us, our homes, and our interactions. Where fear has taken root, we tend to seek two things:

1. A way to avoid experiencing more fear.
2. A way to cope with the fear we already have.

With these goals in mind, we design our lives around fear. We unknowingly create for ourselves systems, behaviors, and attitudes that we believe will minimize the fear we experience and bring us comfort in those times we find ourselves staring fear in the face.

Nowhere is this more true than in the modern home. Yet if ever there was a place where fear should not be present, it's at home. Peace and love should rule in this most intimate of spaces, which we share with our most beloved people. Nevertheless, frequently it is the home where fear is most evident in our lives. In the one place fear should have the least control over us, it often has the most.

> If ever there was a place where fear should not be present, it's at home.

Because fear is driving our decisions, we design our homes from the ground up with this idea that they will protect us. And it all begins with the foundation.

The Foundation of Safety

The foundation of the modern home is *safety*. People who are experiencing fear search for safety. We want to do everything in our power to keep ourselves and those we love safe. While we can make wise choices and save ourselves from some dangers, we cannot fully protect ourselves or others. Let's face it: life in a fallen world is dangerous, and true safety apart from God is an illusion. And ironically, the more we pursue safety, the less safe we feel.

The Roof of Appearances

If the foundation of the modern home is safety, the roof is *appearances*. We believe that if we can project the appearance of success and righteousness, it will eventually lead to the real thing while sheltering us from many ills in life. "Fake it till you make it" is our motto. While we might be able to deceive our neighbors, we can't deceive ourselves for very long. Trying to present ourselves as something we are not is exhausting, and we live in constant fear of being found out.

The Wall of Materialism

The first wall of the modern home is *materialism*. So many of us attempt to find comfort and solace in material things. We think that a nice house, a good car, and fine things will fulfill our desires and exempt us from suffering. We think material things can protect and soothe us during tough times. Of course, they cannot. Not only can material things not save us from suffering, but possessing them actually complicates our lives and adds to our worries and concerns (Ecclesiastes 5:10–15).

The Wall of Power

The second wall of the modern home is *power*. Of course, there's a long history of powerful people building fortunes and empires on the backs of the weak. We may even have personal experience of injustice or scary things that happened because of someone who had power over us or a loved one. We believe that if we were in charge, if we had money and the power it brings, the amount of pain we experience would diminish. While having power might allow us to inflict pain on someone else for a change, it can't keep us from experiencing our own pain.

We're Working with Faulty Materials

The construction materials we use to build our homes are rarely selected with great foresight or consideration. I don't know any husband and wife who have intentionally sat down to have a lengthy discussion about what will form the foundation of their home. Most people live in a constant state of denial, and few take time to consider how they will deal with the inevitable storms of life or what type of roof might best protect them. While we will debate paint colors and floor coverings ad nauseum, we rarely give any thought to what kind of walls will best serve us in the midst of troubling times.

As we build our homes, we do so haphazardly without a plan, sawing, hammering, drilling, and wiring whatever feels right and seems appropriate in the moment. Unfortunately, the structures we erect and depend on to shelter and rescue us are useless and often escalate the anxiety and fear we are trying to avoid. Let's see how this approach worked out the first time around.

It's funny to think that Adam and Eve thought that hiding from God in the bushes would work, let alone make them safe. It didn't.

They tried keeping God from seeing their sin, perhaps thinking He gave a fig about appearances. He didn't.

The trouble all started because they believed the lie that possessing something they didn't have would make their lives better. It didn't.

When confronted with his wrongdoing, Adam blamed Eve in the hope that deflecting responsibility onto her would exempt him from the consequences of his sin. It didn't.

First Family of Fear

It's not only important to see what happened when humanity first put their trust in something other than God; it's vital to take note of *where* it happened. Fear was born into the home of the first family. The place created to be a source of love, support, and safety became defined by fear. When the object of their trust failed, the family members distanced themselves from each other and tried to hide from God and the truth. They failed to take personal responsibility, each downplaying his or her role in the debacle. That's when the finger-pointing started.

But it didn't stop there. Just one generation later, Adam and Eve's oldest son was afraid his true character would be exposed, so to cover himself, he murdered his brother and lied about his crime. While Cain was fully responsible for his own actions, we can fairly assume that he was raised in an environment of fear. He saw it in his exiled parents, as they not only modeled it for him but likely taught him to make decisions from a place of fear. And this cycle of fear and self-destruction has been the standard operating procedure for families ever since.

Fear rules us and rules our homes. Some fears are appropriate and understandable. If we don't have them, we probably aren't paying attention to the realities of life. Yet many of our debilitating fears are unnecessary. They aren't a God-given part of life but are the by-products of placing our trust in the wrong things. And when our idols fail, our fears grow.

How to Counteract Fear

Fear was never supposed to be the defining characteristic of family. Instead, a loving family was intended to be the antidote to counteract fear. The love, support, and emotional connection found in a healthy family were meant to empower us and give us courage.

In a healthy family, a child can take those first tentative steps and begin to explore his world because he knows his parents are watching him.

In a healthy family, a husband and wife can have the difficult conversation because they have promised to love each other for better or worse.

In a healthy family, a parent can face the uncertainty of death because she has created a legacy of love.

While misplaced fears can paralyze us, love for family should motivate us. A healthy family provides such a solid foundation upon which we build our lives that it defines our lives more than any potential danger we might face.

Yet too often, instead of family dispelling fear, fear poisons a family. It prevents us from having hard conversations. It immobilizes us from taking action when needed. We are so terrorized by possible negative outcomes that we fail to engage with the attitudes, behaviors, and expressions of love that would lead to a compelling family life.

So many families are dominated by fear and eventually are destroyed by it.

Fear Not, Love One Another

It's no accident that among the most repeated words in Scripture and the ministry of Christ are some variation of "Fear not" and "Love one another." These two phrases strike at the heart of our modern dilemma. Fear or love—which are we going to follow?

Elisabeth Kübler-Ross, famed grief psychologist and bestselling author, said we cannot feel both fear and love at the same time.[2] They are exclusive reactions. We might be able to shift quickly from one to the other, but we cannot experience both simultaneously. Unknowingly, we choose fear more often than love. In so doing, we begin to overvalue good things and make them into godlike things to be worshipped.

Safety is a good concept. There's nothing wrong with wanting our families to be safe. But when we begin to idolize safety and make it the overriding factor in our decision-making, it becomes a danger to us.

Appearances aren't something we should just ignore or forget. We *should* consider the weight of our names and the reputation of our hearts. However, appearances should not be our primary concern when making parenting decisions.

There's nothing inherently wrong with owning material things. And a person with power and money can effect real change and accomplish great good. However, building our lives on the acquisition of possessions and/or power is like constructing our house on shifting sand. People who idolize these things lie awake at night, wondering when it's all going to come crashing down around them.

The Home of the Afraid

The first verse of "The Star-Spangled Banner" concludes with a question: "O say does that star-spangled banner yet wave / o'er the land of the free and the home of the brave?" These lyrics were taken from a poem written by attorney Francis Scott Key during the War of 1812.

Having met with British naval officers to discuss an exchange of prisoners, Key had overheard their battle plans and was therefore detained and could only watch from the enemy's flagship as, that night, the British fleet bombarded American troops at Baltimore's Fort McHenry. He was overjoyed whenever he caught a glimpse of the fort's flag beneath the red glare of the rockets. But once the shelling stopped, Key had no way of knowing which side had prevailed in the battle—until the morning sun had risen, revealing the Stars and Stripes still proudly waving in dawn's early light.

We continue to sing those words before most American sporting events, but the question has subtly changed over the years. Oh sure, the flag is still waving outside our houses, our churches, and our stadiums. But do we really live in "the home of the brave"? I don't believe we do.

It's more likely we're living in the Home of the Afraid.

Restoring the Home of the Brave

So how do we turn things around? What kind of extreme home makeover will it take to restore the Home of the Brave? Anyone who's taken part in a twelve-step recovery program can tell you that the first step is recognizing that you have a problem. The first half of this book was written to help us do just that. In these chapters, we will delve deeper into our misguided attempts to establish our homes on safety, appearances, materialism, and power. The second half of the book will provide a plan for rebuilding our homes with the reliable, durable materials that God intended.

Clearly, the modern family home needs a major redesign. This begins by replacing fear with love. We must give up our seeming addiction to fear and allow love to dictate our actions and our attitudes. This isn't to say we need to stop feeling fear; no one can truly do that. Sometimes it's perfectly natural to experience fear. What we must do, however, is stop being *led* by fear. We must recognize it, feel it, and then put it in its proper place.

It's okay to let fear into the family minivan, but we don't have to hand it the keys. Fear drives us to make bad decisions that slowly undermine the family. Instead, it's time we put love in the driver's seat. At the very least, love should be our GPS—the guiding principle by which we make every decision.

> It's time we put love
>
> in the driver's seat.

As we allow love to take the place of fear, the Home of the Afraid will gradually be remodeled into the Home of the Brave. But first we need to recognize and admit the presence of fear in our lives. Then we must choose a different way.

Consider:

How would life in your home be different if you stopped making decisions based on fear?

How could a healthy portion of bravery change your parenting style?

What kind of difference might courage play in your marriage?

How might your home benefit if you prioritized emotional strength over physical safety?

What would your home look like if you placed a higher value on truth than on appearances?

What could your family accomplish if you stopped looking for comfort in material things?

What kind of influence could you have in your home and community if you chose biblical submission over the pursuit of power?

Our homes need to become training grounds for faith and courage. We must prioritize bravery in our marriages, our parenting, our finances, and every facet of home life. More than safety, we must value strength. While we should never foolishly place ourselves in danger, we cannot turn safety into a false god. I can't keep my kids safe at all times, but I can assist them in becoming strong so they're able to face any challenge. My marriage can't always be safe, but my wife and I can develop the emotional muscle that allows us to endure whatever life throws at us.

Home is a big word. It's full of power and potential. It's time we remade our homes into sources of courage and strength. But to create the Home of the Brave, we must first understand the Home of the Afraid.

Think on These Things

1. How would you say your home has been defined by fear? How does that fear express itself in the choices you make?
2. Consider fight, flight, or freeze. Which is your primary way to deal with fear? How does this manifest itself in different situations at home?
3. What is preventing your home from becoming a place that drives out fear and motivates each member toward love?
4. How might your home be changed for the better if everyone's choices were based on expressions of love?

Chapter 2

Safety: The Wrong Question I Regularly Ask

Even though I walk through the valley of the shadow of death, I will fear no evil, for you are with me.

Psalm 23:4

Behold, I am sending you out as sheep in the midst of wolves.

Matthew 10:16

Comedian John Mulaney confessed to having been an anxious kid. In a stand-up routine from 2012, Mulaney claimed his anxiety eventually went away because, as an adult, many of his childhood fears proved not to be so dangerous after all. Take quicksand, for example. Quicksand was a real and very present danger in the cartoons he watched as a kid. Yet as an adult, he's never even *seen* quicksand, let alone had to navigate around it while driving on the interstate. Cartoons taught him the three greatest dangers in adult life are quicksand, sticks of dynamite, and an anvil falling from the sky.[1]

He's right that many of the fears we harbored as children never come to fruition. Yet there are many terrifying things about adulthood that we never saw in cartoons.

There was never an episode in which Bugs Bunny has to wait the weekend for biopsy results to show whether the lump in his chest is malignant or benign.

We never saw the Road Runner as a tough, old bird dealing with a nagging hip injury that keeps him from getting around.

As far as I know, Minnie Mouse never walked out on Mickey because she'd developed feelings for Goofy.

And Scooby-Doo didn't know the emotional weight of being a single parent who's trying to pay the bills while also homeschooling his kids because the nation is quarantined during a pandemic.

It may be the greatest misconception of childhood that adulthood is far less scary than being a kid. It's not. That said, we shouldn't downplay the fears of our children. And I certainly don't advocate scaring them straight so they know what they have to look forward to. But it's true that adulthood is frightening in ways we never could have imagined as kids.

My phone shows the security camera feeds from work.

We live on a major street, so I'm tempted to install an automatic gate in my driveway.

Anytime a door opens or a window is raised in my house, a chime sounds to let me know it's happening.

Occasionally, I can't sleep at night until I get up to double-check that I've locked the front door.

When it was time to get a dog, we got a German shepherd. When my kids are in the yard, I want others to know they're not alone.

Nowadays, none of these things are unusual or extreme. They're just the routine precautions we take to make sure our homes are secure.

If you were to ask several parents what hope they have for their children, safety would likely top most of their lists. It makes sense that Maslow's famous hierarchy of needs ranks safety as the second-most important human need, right behind physiological needs such as air, food, and water.

Today, nearly every home is built on a foundation of safety.

The Fear That Is

Fear has been around since the earliest days of mankind. It isn't new. Yet our day is somehow different. While every generation before us has experienced fear, today's family faces a unique threat. Never has fear played such a central role in day-to-day decision-making as it does now. Why is that?

Something unusual happened in the 1990s. As the crime rate inexplicably plummeted, the fear of most Americans dramatically increased. Consider, in the 1990s, the nation's murder rate dropped by 20 percent, but the number of stories about murder on national news shows increased 600 percent![2] As cable news networks grew in popularity, so did the fear of the people watching them. Given their unprecedented need to fill twenty-four hours of news programming every day, CNN and Fox News drifted toward the kinds of stories that pulled in the most viewers, thus increasing ratings and, not coincidentally, ad revenues. What kinds of stories draw the most eyeballs? The ones that scare the audience. Think war, violence, pandemics, natural and man-made disasters. "If it bleeds, it leads," my seventh-grade journalism teacher told us. Political scandal proved to be a big draw as well, even as it undermined our confidence in those who had been placed in power over us. It was true then, and it's true now. So the twenty-four-hour news networks built their programming around dramatic stories and alarming footage, and more and more Americans switched from ingesting news for thirty minutes a day to watching it all day and all night.

Then came 9/11. We watched as international terrorists targeted Americans on live television, and fear became a permanent fixture in our daily lives. Suddenly, it seemed as though terrorists could be anywhere inside our borders, maybe even living next door. The first post-9/11 arrest happened in my hometown of Fort Smith, Arkansas. The man taken into custody turned out to be innocent, but it would take years to find that out. Meanwhile, the nightmarish footage played constantly for weeks and months, confirming our fear that danger was all around us.

All of this was before iPhones and social media. When Steve Jobs put a phone in every pocket in 2007, he gave us access to an unending barrage of shocking news bulletins, delivered directly to the palms of our hands with a pleasant *ding*. Friends, relatives, and complete strangers cooperate with this fearmongering by hitting "share" and forwarding every horrifying headline, startling rumor, and creepy urban legend to our inboxes and news feeds. No generation has ever been bombarded with so much negative information. It's no wonder anxiety is at an all-time high among children and teenagers.[3]

American parents have always pushed their children toward a brighter future, hoping and believing their kids would have it better than they did. But this might be the first generation of parents trying to hold their children back from a darker future instead of pushing them forward into a brighter future. And anxious parents raise anxious children.

> This might be the first generation of parents trying to hold their children back from a darker future instead of pushing them forward into a brighter future.

Our main church campus in Fort Smith was constructed in the days just before security became a major concern. At the time, fire was the primary threat to a building of our size. Architects would design buildings like ours with many points of egress so people could exit as quickly as possible in an emergency. Our preschool rooms were selected based on age: the younger the children, the closer they were placed to the front door. That meant that as soon as you walked in, you could drop off your baby. The toddlers' room was located farther down, while kindergarten classrooms were placed at the end of the hall. This setup was designed to get the smaller children out first.

These days we are in process of renovating the church, and one of the priorities will be getting the babies away from the front door. When parents walk into our preschool classrooms today, they're not thinking, *Oh, good, my baby will be close to the door in case of a fire.* Instead, they are stunned that the infants' space is so accessible to someone who might want to walk in, steal a baby, and make a quick getaway.

Forget that it is virtually unheard of that a stranger walks into a church and steals a baby; parents assume it's a threat. To make them feel more comfortable, we are changing the design of our building. Will this make their children safer? Not significantly. But if parents aren't comfortable, they won't attend our church, so we will spend a great deal of money changing our building.

Asking the Wrong Question

In a post-9/11, post-pandemic world that is perceived as overwhelmingly dangerous, one question is on the minds of many: *Is it safe?* This question is so essential to our culture these days that I struggle to think of a scenario in which it isn't an appropriate question.

As a father, I ask it when making decisions regarding my children. The doctor wants to prescribe a new medication. My son asks about playing football. My daughter wants to spend the night at a friend's house. In each situation, I ask or think, "Is it safe?"

As a pastor, I ask it in reference to our church programs. The children's ministry wants to do a hayride, but I remember reading somewhere that some insurance companies will no longer cover hayrides due to the risk of injury. The student ministry is organizing a program that includes kids being blindfolded and pushed in carts. The missions team is headed to a Third World country that has been in the news because of violence in the streets. In each situation, as a leader who has responsibilities for those involved, I ask, "Is it safe?"

My wife wants to fly an airline with a bad reputation.

My realtor is showing me a home in a different neighborhood.

My electrician found a "unique" way to do what I've asked.

In each situation, I ask, "Is it safe?"

The question is sound, prudent, and rational. It's a question we *should* ask regularly. Someone who never asks the question is likely irresponsible, reckless, and a possible danger to themselves and others.

However, this should not be the question driving our lives and everyday choices. It's a fair question to ask, but it should never be the primary question.

Jesus Never Did

Jesus loved to ask questions. In many situations, He used a teaching technique much like the Socratic method, in which He asked His listeners questions to expose flaws in their logic. Questions cause people to think, forcing them to reexamine their beliefs. Jesus asked questions, not because He didn't know the answer, but because He wanted to help people arrive at the truth themselves.

It's striking to me that the question I ask all the time is one that Jesus never asked. He never concerned Himself with personal safety or asked His disciples to consider their safety before doing His will. Some might wrongly conclude that He never raised the question because following God's will is always the safe thing to do, but they would be wrong. Much of what God calls us to do is decidedly *unsafe* in earthly terms. How many people have been persecuted for worshipping Christ? How many have been imprisoned and tortured for preaching Jesus in China, North Korea, Iran, Somalia, and other lands hostile to Christianity? How many missionaries have been injured or killed taking the gospel to the ends of the earth? How many men and women have been martyred for refusing to renounce their Christian beliefs?

The fact is, Jesus never asked the question because safety is not as much of a priority for Him as it is for us. From His perspective, there are other questions far more pressing.

Is it right?
Is it true?
Is it noble?
Is it loving?
Is it glorifying to God?
Is it obedient?

The answers to these questions are far more important than whether we are safely tucked into our warm, comfortable beds every night.

When faced with the choice of whether to continue holding regular public worship services during the COVID-19 pandemic of 2020, the decision didn't come down to "What is the safest choice for our people?" Instead, we asked ourselves, "What is the most loving choice we can make for our neighbors' sake?" We decided it would be unloving to meet and risk spreading the virus, possibly leading to a neighbor's illness or even death. Love, not safety, was the most important question.

Again, it's not wrong to consider the safety factor when making a decision. We should never recklessly put our lives on the line; we've been given a desire to live for a reason. God doesn't expect us to *seek out* persecution or suffering.

However, the desire to keep ourselves and our families safe should not be the driving force for our lives. Certainly, we should never equate safety with God's will, because then we equate risk with being outside God's will. And if there is anything the history of God's people has shown us, it is that God often calls us to do risky, unsafe things.

> We should never equate safety with God's will, because then we equate risk with being outside God's will.

When safety is our primary concern, obedience will not be our primary response to God.

The Pursuit of the Unattainable

It's never been safer to be a child than it is today. For one thing, the child mortality rate in the United States has dropped by more than 93 percent since 1935. A good portion of the decrease can be attributed to the rise in childhood vaccinations. A number of major diseases have been eliminated or are treatable because of vaccination programs.[4]

Between 1993 and 2013, the number of child pedestrians struck and killed by automobiles fell by more than two-thirds. Child homicides are way down, as are child abductions. In fact, for a kid between the ages of five and fourteen today, the chances of premature death by any means are roughly one-tenth of one percent.[5]

Nearly every major statistic has shown an increase in safety for kids. Yet parents don't feel as though their children are safer. In his book *Generation Z Unfiltered: Facing Nine Hidden Challenges of the Most Anxious Population*, author Tim Elmore pointed out that, in parenting, perception is often reality, and a majority of parents believe there's never been a more *dangerous* time to be a child. This leads to an abundance of caution from parents. Rather than empowering their children to navigate difficult situations, parents go out of their way to protect their children from *ever experiencing any risk*. These parents are "preparing the path for the child instead of the child for the path."[6]

Yes, parents should be discerning. It's wise for parents to set reasonable boundaries, know who their kids' friends are, and occasionally review their children's phones (which the parents pay for) and online activity. However, parents must realize that they desire a safety for their kids they simply cannot fully secure, and that this desire is leading them to behaviors and decisions that will in no way better their children's lives. It's not discerning for parents to hover over their children ("helicopter parenting") or to meticulously plan out their kids' days ("snowplow parenting") so their children don't miss out on something or to steer their kids clear from emotional discomfort. It's fear, not good parenting, that is causing today's parents to micromanage their children.

Okay, you might ask, what about the dangerous world we adults deal with every day? Let's talk about that. Did you know the violent crime rate in America is less than half of what it was twenty-five years ago? Yet the majority of Americans believe crime is increasing.[7] We live in a much safer society than we did a few decades ago, but safety has not lessened our fears. If the safety we crave promises to end our fears, has it produced what it promised? Isn't it interesting that many experts say there has never been a more anxious time to be alive? We are both safer *and* more afraid.

Our modern lives are often built on the foundation of safety with the expectation that if we can make our lives more and more safe, our fears will have less and less influence over us. Yet our fears have only escalated. Despite a modern social acceptance of mental health issues, an increase in availability of professional counseling, a plethora of self-help books being published every year, a preponderance of information available via the internet, and a sharp rise in medications being prescribed for anxiety, we are still a frightened people.

Of course, just because we are unable to attain a completely safe life doesn't keep us from attempting to do so. We think that if we can ever *be* safe, we will *feel* safe. Our anxiety will just fade away. And so we build the foundations of our lives on safety, and it becomes the defining factor that determines all things. If something isn't safe, it doesn't belong. We demand safe lives with safe kids in safe homes. Only after our safety is ensured can we even begin to think about everything else we want in our lives.

But the truth is, we can never be completely safe. We are building our homes on foundations that cannot stand. Instead of decreasing or eliminating our fears, our obsession with safety is actually increasing our angst.

Idolizing Safety

Pursuing safety seems natural and right. After all, if we're not safe, then we're not free to do all the other good things we want to accomplish. However, when we take something good, like safety, and value it more than we should, it often leads to negative consequences. Prioritizing (read: idolizing) safety can cause us to make and excuse poor choices, avoid intimacy and expressions of love, physically and emotionally hide, and blame others for our mistakes.

The decision-making process generally involves proposing more than one possible course of action and then examining the pros and cons, advantages and disadvantages, and right and wrong of each option available to us. When we make an idol of safety, we assume that any choice that appears to be at odds with our physical or emotional well-being must be the wrong choice. The problem is that the safe choice is often the wrong choice, while the right choice often entails risk.

Not every opportunity to serve is safe. For example, it wasn't safe for Father Damien or Mother Teresa to care for lepers, but it was the right thing to do.

It's not safe for a firefighter to run into a burning building to rescue a child, but it's the right thing to do.

When people hurt you with their words or actions, it may not feel safe to swallow your pride and pain and forgive them, but it's the Christlike thing to do.

It's not emotionally safe for a husband or wife to initiate a difficult conversation about parenting or sex or the household budget. You're risking a possibly unpleasant confrontation and upsetting the status quo. But in many circumstances it is the right and necessary choice to start the discussion.

Overvaluing safety in our homes and lives empowers and excuses us to avoid intimacy and love. By sheer definition, love isn't safe. When we love, we willfully choose to do what is in the best interest of the other person no matter what his or her response might be. We make ourselves vulnerable to possible rejection and pain. This isn't safe, but it is right. However, when we build our lives and homes on a foundation of safety, we think anything that involves vulnerability, uncertainty, or the potential for pain is wrong and, therefore, a poor choice.

Ask parents if they love their children, and most will quickly say yes. They are willing to prove their love by sacrificing their lives for the sake of their children, an action that is clearly not safe. But do we truly love our children as much as we think? Although I might be ready to lay down my life for my kids in an emergency situation, am I also ready to allow them to dislike me when I make an unpopular parenting decision? Are you willing to deal with your child's public tantrum by taking appropriate, loving disciplinary action, even if it means drawing attention to the fact that your family isn't perfect? Many so value their reputations that they would choose to appease the child and give him what he wants to keep him from making a scene.

Love is not always neat. It's oftentimes scary and rife with potential outcomes we do not desire. Fear offers a different deal. It promises us security, a lack of vulnerability, and more specific desirable outcomes. Of course, fear rarely produces what it promises, but it does give a good sales pitch. Love isn't so skilled. From the get-go it lets you know that things might not go the way you wish. When we value safety first, love rarely seems like the right thing to do.

Consider Adam. When he was about to be confronted with his sin, he made a choice to run from God. The only way to justify this foolish act as being the right move is that Adam thought it was safe. Or safer. He then attempted to blame his wife for his poor choices. When safety is our god, we try to justify just about any action as long as we think that doing so might protect us. Instead of stepping up and sacrificing himself out of love for his wife, Adam used her to excuse his poor choices because of his affection for safety. He physically and emotionally hid and cast blame on another.

Adam Hid and So Do We

When Adam felt fear, his first response was to hide. As God came walking through the garden, Adam ran from His presence and took cover behind some trees. Adam had no desire to face the consequences of his actions or reveal the fallen condition of his soul. He didn't want to be seen.

This is often our response to fear as well. We look for a place to hide.

How do we hide?

1. We physically avoid uncomfortable or inconvenient situations. One of the most common ways we hide is simply by staying clear of a particular place so we won't have to deal with certain issues.

During a time of reflection after my grandmother had died, I realized that I hadn't gone to visit her at home the last few days before she was taken to the hospital. She lived next door, and I was often at her house multiple times every day. Part of the reason I didn't see her those final days was that she wasn't feeling well, and I didn't want to bother her, especially with my kids in tow. But chances are, I also subconsciously knew things were not good and I was avoiding difficult circumstances, as many of us do. I was hiding.

There are some places we are just supposed to be, and sometimes we seek safety by not being in those places. For example:

Many workaholics don't actually *like* work; they just like to work more than they like being at home. They are hiding.

A lot of parents—usually mom *or* dad, not both—spend every other weekend traveling with a child who's participating in "travel ball." A good number of these parents are there because they would rather be on the road than at home with their wife or husband. They are hiding.

We can talk about how times have changed and what constitutes regular attendance these days, but one aspect of the decline in church attendance in America is that if we don't show up, we don't have to confess or give or serve. Some people choose not to attend church because they are hiding.

2. We hide emotionally. Sometimes we can't avoid situations physically, but we can avoid them emotionally. We can be present physically but absent emotionally. We erect walls around our hearts so our true feelings and emotions won't be exposed.

When asked our opinions, we might tell the people asking what they want to hear rather than revealing our true beliefs. Or we might shade our opinions or shrug off the question, giving the impression that something isn't as important to us as it actually is.

The word *fine* is often a form of emotional hiding. A friend or spouse can tell something is wrong, so she asks you how you are, and you respond, "Fine." You're hiding. Afraid to tell the truth, you mask it behind a single-word response meant to fend off follow-up questions.

Other times we will completely avoid topics or conversations. It's one thing to dodge a conversation that you know will cause tension but not resolve anything; choosing not to talk of politics with your crazy uncle at Christmas dinner is probably wise. But avoiding a discussion with your wife or husband regarding a prickly issue that is hurting your marriage? That is not wise.

3. Addiction is often a way of hiding. Rather than dealing with our pain, loneliness, or frustrations, we mask our hurt with destructive behaviors—alcohol, pills, sex, work, or whatever our form of addiction might be. When the inevitable negative consequences begin to manifest, instead of dealing with the problem, we turn again to our addiction of choice to dull the pain.

4. The blame game is a form of hiding. Denying responsibility for our bad choices and shifting the blame to others is another common way to hide. Some of us believe our failures are the fault of our parents. Others blame our bosses for holding us back or our coworkers for not doing their jobs. We blame our spouses for our unhappiness and our political opponents for the ills of our country. It's all hiding.

Hiding Does Not Work

Hiding didn't work for Adam, and it won't work for us either. While it might give us a brief sense of safety in the moment, it will not suffice to protect us for the long haul. Instead, hiding hinders us in three major ways.

- **Fear of getting caught.** In many cases, the fear of getting caught is just as bad, if not worse, than the fear that caused us to hide in the first place. Like a liar who must always be careful so that his lies are not exposed, hiding requires us to make an extra effort to continually conceal our issues or feelings. It's exhausting, and the weariness makes us even more susceptible to fear.

- **Isolation.** Few things are lonelier than hiding. We can be in the midst of a large crowd but feel completely alone if we're actively hiding something from others. Not only do we feel lonely in our secrets, but that loneliness makes us more prone to fear. Remember as a kid what it was like to lie alone in the darkness at night compared to when you had a friend spend the night or a parent was in your room? Everything is scarier when you're alone, and hiding makes us feel more alone.

- **Loss of time.** Hiding causes us to become stuck. Had God left Adam to his own devices, he probably would have stayed hidden in the trees for the rest of his life. His life would've been put on hold because of one (admittedly very big) mistake. It was tremendous love on God's part that called Adam out from hiding and into the light. I'm sure it didn't feel like love to Adam, but it was in fact love. Whenever we choose to hide, it's as though time stands still. We can't grow, we can't learn, and we can't move past our issues. Instead, we get stuck. When you and I hide in our addictions, or hide our grief or hurt or shame, we end up going nowhere fast.

The Question I Should Be Asking

Rather than asking, "Is it safe?" the question I need to ask is this: "Am I using safety as an excuse not to love?"

My abundance of caution is often simply a way of avoiding what needs to be done. Because picking up the phone and calling a friend I may have hurt carries with it the threat of emotional tension and possible rejection, I don't make the phone call. I've allowed my personal safety to trump love.

While I want to protect my children, if I don't teach them to navigate this world, I will actually be placing them in greater danger. So I need to push them toward taking risks, toward finding answers on their own, toward overcoming hurts when they happen. Sometimes it is wiser to let them experience a few bumps and bruises and hold them after they've been hurt.

I want to protect my marriage. But even if my marriage is struggling, seeking professional help carries with it a great deal of emotional risk. If I overvalue safety, I won't seek the help we need because I'm not willing to be vulnerable, submit to change, or confront the pain I might have caused or experienced. However, if I recognize the pitfalls of playing it safe and instead choose the way of love, I will do whatever it takes to improve my marriage.

Again, safety *is* an important consideration in life. But it has become the primary lens through which we view every decision. The plain truth, however, is that our lives are not nearly in the danger we often think they are. Our pursuit of safety is not protecting our families or saving our lives; it's keeping us from living our lives to the fullest.

When we focus primarily on love rather than safety, we often get both. But when we fixate on safety at the expense of love, we often get neither.

Think on These Things

1. How much does a desire for safety influence your decisions?

2. Identify a time in your marriage or parenting when you allowed safety to trump love. What were the results?

3. Before reading the statistics in this chapter, did you believe the world was safer or more dangerous today than it was thirty years ago? How did this belief impact your actions?

4. Identify an area in your life in which you may be hiding. What is one concrete step you can take right now to come out of hiding?

Chapter 3

Appearances: A Bad Umbrella

Woe to you, scribes and Pharisees, hypocrites! For you are like
whitewashed tombs, which outwardly appear beautiful, but
within are full of dead people's bones and all uncleanness.
So you also outwardly appear righteous to others, but
within you are full of hypocrisy and lawlessness.

Matthew 23:27–28

Nevertheless, many even of the authorities believed
in him, but for fear of the Pharisees they did not
confess it ... for they loved the glory that comes from
man more than the glory that comes from God.

John 12:42–43

The rains are going to come. There's no stopping them. We might be able to pack up the family and move to a corner of the world with less annual rainfall, but try as we might, we cannot control the clouds. When it comes to the troubles of life, we can make wise choices and possibly experience fewer storms than others, but we can't completely exclude them from our lives. As Longfellow put it, "Thy fate is the common fate of all, into each life some rain must fall."[1]

The rains are going to come. A child with autism. The loss of a job. Betrayal by a loved one. Grief. Failure. Money problems. Cancer. Aging. Life is full of difficulties. No matter what we do, our lives will occasionally take a turn we didn't expect and don't desire. Sometimes when it rains, it pours. And so we seek refuge under something, and the shelter we often run toward first is that of keeping up appearances.

We think that if we can maintain an aura of strength, competency, and completeness in the face of adversity that maybe we can ward off anything that might cause us fear. We somehow convince ourselves that the umbrella of appearances will minimize the pain we experience in this life.

Survival of the Fittest

If modern life were a nature documentary, it would be narrated by Oscar-winning actor Morgan Freeman, his voice brimming with compassion and gravitas: "We limp through life at our own peril. In this survival-of-the-fittest world, we must be careful with whom we share our struggles and scars. Weakness is a threat to our survival. With potential predators all around, we must project health and power, or we become targets. In the animal kingdom, lions attack the weakest zebra. It's the crippled gazelle that is dinner for hyenas. On the streets of the city, as on the savanna, the wounded animal is a dead animal."

That's how most of us approach life, as though something is stalking us, waiting to take us down at the first sign of weakness.

And so we hide behind appearances. We fear that any feebleness or injury or struggle we reveal to others is only setting up our downfall. So we pretend, lie, deceive, project, and do everything in our power to appear to be something we are not, all in an attempt to protect ourselves and alleviate our fears.

When my daughter was young, it was easy for me to know when she was lying. I would ask her a question that I already knew the answer to. She would put a hand over her mouth and tell me what she thought I wanted to hear. "Did you eat the cookie?" I'd ask. "No," she'd say, hand over her mouth. "Did you brush your teeth?" I'd ask. "Yes," she'd say, hand over her mouth.

Ella thought that as long as she told me what I wanted to hear, I wouldn't be able to recognize her lies. She thought the appearance of truth was the same thing as truth. It's not, of course, but it's cute when a child thinks it so. It's not so cute when adults do the same.

Since the garden of Eden, people have believed that if they can create and maintain the appearance of success and virtue and goodness, no one will see through their veneer and recognize their true nature. The worst of us believe that appearances are, in fact, all that really matter. They will do everything in their power to preserve their facades, with no intention of ever becoming the virtuous people they project publicly. Some of us have slightly better intentions. We believe that if we can just keep up appearances to buy time, eventually—with effort—we can become inwardly the people we profess to be outwardly. While the latter fakery may be slightly nobler than the former, neither is sufficient to alleviate our anxiety.

Seeking refuge in appearances only creates more fear, because we know that at any moment, our actual condition could be revealed and everything would fall apart. That's why appearances make a lousy umbrella. They cannot protect us from adversity. The fact is, they hinder our ability to face the truth and deal with difficult times.

When Daniel asked me to lunch, I assumed he had another business venture he wanted to discuss. Though highly successful at his profession, Daniel would occasionally call me to get my thoughts on his next project. But as this lunch got started, I could tell something else was on his mind.

To outsiders, Daniel and Jennifer seem to have it all together. Their kids are beautiful, their businesses are successful, and while not perfect, they are stellar people. But everyone has issues, so it was no surprise to me when Daniel began to talk about a struggle within their marriage. He loved Jennifer, but she had recently come across a couple of his texts with another woman. Nothing physical had happened, but the texts were inappropriate.

It's a conversation I have all the time, and I was happy Daniel had reached out to me. As we continued to talk, I offered a few suggestions, but it quickly became apparent that seeking advice was not the point of our meeting. In fact, Daniel didn't want help; he was trying to appease Jennifer. She had found the texts, confronted him, and demanded action, and so he agreed to see me. He wasn't willing to do anything more. He could accept that I knew about his mistakes, but he wasn't prepared for anyone else to know. When I suggested couples counseling, Daniel downplayed the seriousness of the situation and waved off my suggestion as unnecessary. He didn't want to confront his problems; he wanted to give Jennifer the *appearance* that he was facing them.

Daniel's thinking isn't difficult to understand. Imagine living in a rural town where everybody knows everyone else. There's one restaurant, one stoplight, and one main road. In a little strip mall off the main road, a marriage counselor keeps an office where, one day a week, she holds appointments after driving in from a neighboring town. Now imagine your marriage hits a roadblock. You still love each other, and you don't want a divorce. But life is busy, raising kids is difficult, and you've lost that spark you once had. You call the counselor and ask about an appointment. The only opening she has is at noon on Tuesday, and you know that during the lunch hour everybody will see your car parked in front of the counselor's office.

Do you make the appointment?

Fear says no. Fear tells you that everyone will know, that before the first session has ended, the small-town rumor mill will already be at work. Your mom will know, as will your mother-in-law. Fear says that before you get back to the office, people there will be speculating about the problem you and your spouse are having.

I regularly counsel people to get professional help for their problems, but they often refuse because they're worried about what others might think. They are more concerned with maintaining appearances than fixing their problems. They prefer the mirage of health to actual health.

The Danger of Appearances

There is nothing inherently wrong with outward appearances. Desiring a good name or building a strong reputation is a worthwhile goal. According to the Bible, "a good name is to be chosen rather than great riches, and favor is better than silver or gold" (Proverbs 22:1). The apostle Paul wrote that an overseer of the church "must be well thought of by outsiders, so that he may not fall into disgrace" (1 Timothy 3:7). When outward appearances reflect the true nature of a person, they are useful.

Problems arise, however, when we devote our energy to cultivating appearances instead of working to develop real nobility and good character. We do this because fear tells us we need to seek the approval and admiration of others, regardless of our true nature. The danger is that overvaluing our image doesn't just give a false impression; it hinders our ability to grow.

I deeply desire for my son to have the courage to admit what he doesn't know. If he is in math class and the teacher asks for a volunteer to come to the board to work a problem, it would be wise for him to volunteer so he can see whether he is truly grasping the concepts. If he's not, the teacher is there to point out where he went wrong and lead him to find the right answer. Yet I know that won't be his approach. I know because *no one* approaches math that way in school. Students duck their heads, avert their eyes, and do everything in their power not to be called on when they're unsure of the answer.

I remember when I was a kid and the teacher would call students to the front of the class, I learned to volunteer for one of the first problems because it was always the easiest. I gave the appearance of confidence, but in reality I was trying to duck the harder questions that were sure to come. I would quickly answer my problem, and everyone would assume I fully understood all the concepts. I didn't. But I knew how to work the system.

If only my son could have the courage to ignore what others think of him, risk being wrong, and admit when he needs help, he could learn math much more effectively than I did. But he won't. Why? Because fear tells him not to. It teaches him to pretend to know the answers, thereby avoiding a situation in which his ignorance might be revealed.

Fear tells us the same thing. That's why a couple struggling in marriage chooses not to get help from a counselor. It's why parents who can't figure out how to effectively discipline their teenager will never read a parenting book. It's why individuals who are feeling disconnected or lonely won't reach out to a friend to share their struggles. Fear tells us we can't let our guards down. We must pretend to have it all, know it all, and be it all.

> Fear tells us we can't let our guards down. We must pretend to have it all, know it all, and be it all.

This opens the door to many vices that tend to fall into one of two categories—denial or deceit.

Denial Must Die

One of the first hospital visits I made as a pastor was to an elderly member who was just days away from death. The only problem was, she didn't know it. As soon as I arrived at the hospital, I knew things weren't right. Several family members were standing outside her room, and I asked them for an update. "She only has days to live," one said. I understood and prepared to have possibly my last conversation with the woman. But as I entered the room, the family member added, "We've decided not to tell her. We don't think she can take it."

I froze. My mind flooded with thoughts.

What gives you the right to conceal this from her?

What kind of doctor tells a patient's family she has days to live but doesn't tell the patient, even though she is alert and in full possession of her faculties?

What do you mean by "she can't take it"? What's the worst that could happen—the news might kill her?

I thought all those things, but I said none of them. This family's dysfunction wasn't my business. As a pastor, I had a certain responsibility as the woman's shepherd, but I had no authority to make medical decisions for her. My responsibility was to love her well and tend to her spiritual needs. So I quietly walked into the room and engaged my friend and congregant in a spiritual conversation.

Unless there was more to the story than I knew, the family didn't withhold the truth from their mom because *she* couldn't take it; they failed to tell her because *they* couldn't take it. It's understandable. No one wants to confront the truth that someone they have loved for so long is going to die. But what they did was unfair. Had their mother been functioning at a reduced mental capacity, then their decision might have been valid. But since she was fully capable of making her own choices, they should have told her the truth.

Yes, it would have been difficult. It would have demanded something from them they had probably never experienced. But do you know who could have comforted them? Their mother. The woman of faith I had known likely would have processed the news and then accepted it. She could have shared those last few days with them, talking, loving, making a few more memories. Maybe her family would have heard a story they never heard before. Perhaps she would have told them some things she wished she had done differently or said something she had always meant to say—something that might have made a difference for someone who needed to hear it.

Somewhere along the way, this woman's children learned that denial was an acceptable approach to dealing with distressing news or prickly family issues. Instead of talking through their problems and resolving unpleasant feelings in a healthy manner, they learned to pretend that their problems and unpleasant feelings simply didn't exist. But ignoring uncomfortable truths is a certain path to emotional and relational death.

Yes, in the short term, denial is decidedly more comfortable than confrontation. It takes less effort and creates less immediate pain. But denial comes at a much higher cost in the end, so we must change course and take the hard steps of seeking the truth, telling the truth, and living by the truth. The truth might be more demanding in the short term, but it will bring life in the long run.

The Deceit of Deceit

Sometimes, clinging to appearances can cause us to live in denial of our true state and make bad choices based on our delusion. Other times, we make poor choices for the purpose of deceiving others by projecting an image that has little basis in fact.

Instead of renting or buying a home that fits our family's needs and budget, we overextend ourselves to purchase a five-bedroom, four-bathroom status symbol. Rather than buying a car we like to drive, we purchase one that drives itself to let others know we are financially secure. Couples loudly proclaim their love for each other in public but sleep in separate rooms and hardly speak when they're at home. Parents continually boast about their child on social media but just can't bring themselves to say "I'm proud of you" to the child's face.

Projecting a false or misleading image—pretending to be something we are not—is accomplished by practicing some rather unsavory skills:

Lying

Denial is when we lie to ourselves; deceit is when we lie to others. We justify these lies by telling ourselves that it's not worth the time to explain the truth, and besides, we aren't hurting anyone else. But every lie comes with a price. Lying destroys intimacy and has an erosive effect on our relationships. Ironically, we often lie because we think it will *help* our relationships; we think people like our false selves better than our true selves. So to keep up appearances, we avoid the truth.

Hypocrisy

The origin of hypocrisy is found in ancient theater, where men put on masks to pretend to be something they were not. This is what happens when we set out to deceive—we project an appearance that does not match the reality of our circumstances. Hypocrisy creates tremendous internal tension, causing us to work ever harder to maintain public perceptions while increasing our fear that we're going to be found out.

Selfishness

When we value appearances over everything else, we can't seem to help but think ourselves superior to everyone else. A good amount of projecting an appearance is accomplished by making comparisons, so to elevate ourselves in the eyes of another, we diminish the good qualities of a third party while highlighting that person's faults.

Exaggeration

In keeping up appearances, it's not what is real that matters; it's what we convince others to *believe* is real. Hence, the value of exaggeration and manipulation. We don't have to lie outright if we can just *stretch* the truth, maybe minimize our problems, and overstate our successes. In the end, however, we will do whatever it takes to get others to believe the best about us.

Trans-Affluence

A few years ago, people were shocked to learn that the thirty-seven-year-old African American president of the NAACP chapter in Spokane, Washington, was actually the blonde, white daughter of a Caucasian couple in Montana.

When Rachel Dolezal was exposed as having deceived the public and her employers about her race, intentionally misleading others and knowingly allowing media outlets to misdescribe her ethnic background, Dolezal defended her actions by describing herself as "transracial." Taking a term commonly used to describe an adoption involving parents and children of different races, Dolezal attempted to use it to defend her actions. In a *Today* show interview, she said,

"I identify as black." To most, including the media, her claim was outlandish.[2] Even those who support the idea of "gender fluidity" rejected out of hand the notion that one can simply choose to be of a different race.

While we have many choices open to us in a free society, we can't go on pretending to be something we are not. (At least, not for long.) Yet seeking refuge in appearances tempts us to do just that.

One of the most common symptoms of a society that idolizes appearances is debt. While debt can be useful—it allows a young family to buy a home, a student to further his education, an entrepreneur to start her own company—it's often misused to deceive ourselves and others regarding our true financial condition. Most debt is a symptom of valuing appearances over reality. Not all, but most. Rather than living within the confines of our resources, we spend and pretend. We deny the long-term reality of loan and credit card payments in order to enjoy the immediate benefits of whatever material item we desire, such as a fine house, a luxury car, stylish clothing, and so on. Because we so value appearances, we are willing to go into serious debt. Just as Dolezal pretended to be of a race she was not, many people pretend to be of a socioeconomic status they are not. These people are attempting to be "trans-affluent."

Most debt is a symptom of valuing

appearances over reality.

Many of us identify as people of wealth, even when our bank statements and retirement accounts reveal no evidence to that effect. We project the appearance of affluence, but it's a mirage built on debt and deception. When you aren't paying for what you are possessing, you are trans-affluent. You are pretending to be something you are not.

Far too many are afflicted with this condition. The 2008 recession exposed American trans-affluence on a mass scale. As property values plummeted, it was revealed that many of us owed more money on our homes than the homes were worth. Did people learn from the experience? Apparently not. Twelve years later, when the markets crashed again, Americans were found to be almost as cash-poor and overleveraged as they had been in 2008.

Remodeled homes, luxury cars, recreational boats, designer accessories, trendy gadgets—a lot of Americans possess many things but own very few of them. Instead of aggressively attacking personal debt and saving for retirement, too many people continue to use credit cards to give the appearance of affluence they will never actually possess.

The remedy for trans-affluence is simple: live an authentic life.

Don't pretend to be something you are not.

As Dave Ramsey would say, "Act your wage."[3] Accept your current financial restraints and live within them. If you don't like your current income, let your frustration motivate you to work toward changing your circumstances. But whatever you do, do not attempt to project a wealthy lifestyle when you lack the funds to truly live that life. Remember Warren Buffett's dictum: "If you buy things you do not need, soon you will have to sell things you need."[4]

Our national debt, a good amount of organizational debt, and much of our personal debt—all are by-products of fear. We are afraid, and we're looking for protection and relief from appearances to lessen our anxiety. Either through denial or deceit, we use debt to create a perception that does not match the reality of our situation.

Truth Moves

The truth moves us. We grow as individuals and families when we confront the truth and talk about what is real. Our faults, failures, insecurities, inabilities, and other uncomfortable realities each provide us the opportunity to change course, learn, grow, and adapt. But when we refuse to engage and interact with the truth, we don't move.

There is a simple test to determine if denial and/or deceit are at play in your family: if either is present, you become stuck in place.

When we live in denial, we never confront the truth, and so we cannot be changed by it. We just continue down the same destructive path of action or inaction, believing that nothing is wrong.

When we live in deceit, we have to keep up appearances that all is well, and so we cannot change course. We must continue pretending that we have everything together lest someone realize we've been lying the whole time.

Confronting the truth is what precipitates change. When we give up our desire to maintain appearances and instead embrace the truth, we grow. Parents learn new skills. Children mature. Families navigate challenges and overcome them. Marriages become healthier.

But as long as we care more about what other people think than about how things really are, we will remain stuck.

The Exhaustion of It All

The irony of being stuck is that it's exhausting. It takes a lot of work to go nowhere. Whether we're fooling others or fooling ourselves, the pressure to perform wears us out. It's especially wearisome to keep our aim perpetually on the moving target that is the approval of others.

Many people believe they're exhausted because the pace of modern life is such that they are always busy. What they fail to recognize is that their busyness is just another attempt to keep up appearances. There is no higher badge of honor in modern life than the badge of busyness. It excuses poor choices, keeps others at a distance, and deceives us into believing that we cannot live any other way.

In reality, we are busy because we're afraid. We fear what slowing down might reveal—to us, to our loved ones, to the people whose envy and respect we covet. We think that by staying busy, we can live in denial of the deterioration of our homes and relationships, not to mention our hearts. If we don't slow down, maybe we can deceive others into believing that we have it all together or that we're too important or indispensable to take a break. At the very least, we can earn a little sympathy for how hard we work.

The Truth Is Risky

It's no accident that when we build our lives on the false foundation of safety, the blueprints for our lives naturally call for a roof of appearances. Being accepted by others makes us feel safe. We believe that if other people accept and approve of us, we will be more likely to experience emotional and physical security.

The truth is often risky. Admitting our mistakes, our faults, or our struggles carries with it the possibility that people might use these things against us. The more they know about our actual situations, the more they will be in a position to abuse us, manipulate us, expose us, or turn others against us. Those are risks we're not willing to take. So we continue to reinforce the roof of appearances, believing it to be our safest move, despite all evidence to the contrary.

The Home of the Afraid is taking shape, but this house needs walls. For our first wall, what's more natural to conjoin our desires for safety and appearances than with the false promises of materialism?

Think on These Things

1. How important to you is your reputation in the community? What about at church? How about within your own family?

2. What are some things you don't want other people to know about you or your family? What are some things you've done or said to encourage a favorable but false impression of you or your family?

3. Think of a stress-inducing situation at home that you have been ignoring or avoiding. What are you afraid will happen if you confront the person involved? How might your home be different if you were to confront this problem and resolve it?

4. What is an expensive item you've purchased that you didn't need and couldn't really afford? (Hint: check your past credit card statements.) What are some safeguards you can implement to protect your family from trans-affluence?

Chapter 4

Materialism: To Have More Is to Fear More

Take care, and be on your guard against all covetousness, for one's life does not consist in the abundance of his possessions.

Luke 12:15

But those who desire to be rich fall into temptation, into a snare, into many senseless and harmful desires that plunge people into ruin and destruction. For the love of money is a root of all kinds of evils.

1 Timothy 6:9–10

One of the primary measures of the stock market is volatility. Markets aren't always guided by rational behavior, as investors rarely take a disciplined approach with their money, understanding long-term objectives and making wise choices. Instead, investors are often driven by irrational ideas, which can lead to foolish decisions. Economic situations rarely change in dramatic fashion over forty-eight hours, yet in the last year, we have seen the Dow Jones average post record losses one day and record gains the next.[1] Companies didn't fundamentally change in those two days; the feelings of investors are what caused these massive swings.

The Volatility Index, often called the "fear index," represents an attempt to gauge the current feelings of investors in order to predict volatility in the market over the next thirty days. In some scenarios, investors might be feeling more peaceful, in which case there is a small chance of a significant swing one way or the other in the days and weeks to come. At other times, investors might be feeling uncertain or emotionally on edge, in which case there is a greater likelihood of wild swings in either direction.

Two factors—fear and greed—drive volatility in the stock market. Warren Buffett famously said that investors should be "fearful when others are greedy and greedy when others are fearful."[2]

Fear and greed are kissing cousins. Both are self-centered emotions that cloud our ability to reason correctly and often lead to highly irrational behaviors. They aren't the same thing, but they are deeply related. Fear leads to avoidance, while greed is based on attraction. Fear seeks to protect what we have, while greed seeks to add to what is already ours. Fear is a response to a threat, while greed is a response to a perceived opportunity.

Either is an understandable response in certain moments, but neither provides us with reliable information for making good decisions. In fact, left unchecked, fear and greed can prove fatal.

It's going on forty years since Madonna sang about living in a material world, with a reminder to the boys that she's a material girl.[3] Many of my younger friends don't even know who Madonna is. Those of us who do now feel old. To be fair, I don't remember "Material Girl" Madonna; that was just before my time. I remember "Vogue" Madonna.

While there were much better songs released in the 1980s, probably no song defined the culture of the time like "Material Girl." The song is about a young woman who craves the finer things in life and is willing to manipulate men to get them. Looking back on the '80s—the days of big hair and parachute pants, junk bonds and Gordon Gekko, yuppies and *Lifestyles of the Rich and Famous*—the decade is synonymous with excess, greed, and conspicuous consumption.

But nearly four decades later, are we any less materialistic?

For my generation, which came to awareness in the 1980s, we have never known another way. But the insatiable desire for money and possessions wasn't invented in the '80s. People have struggled with greed throughout history. Long before we lusted after Lamborghinis, Jesus talked about the dangers of longing for wealth and possessions (Luke 12:15–21). But thanks in part to revolutionary developments in media, marketing, and mass production over the past hundred or so years, mankind is more tempted than ever to look for meaning in material things.

The Wall of Materialism

The Home of the Afraid has two primary walls connecting the foundation of safety to the roof of appearances. We put up walls to keep dangers out, but these walls are unstable because fear and greed drive their construction. Volatility is definitely high in this house. The first of these two walls is the wall of materialism.

There is a distinct relationship between the wall of materialism, the foundation of safety, and the roof of appearances. It's our disproportionate desire for safety that tells us to value money and possessions. Those few who have a proper view of safety—a belief that we should make prudent choices but with a complete awareness that we can never fully secure safety for ourselves—understand that money is a tool to be used and not a god to be worshipped. They recognize the dangers of loving money and take measures to protect their hearts from greed.

When we overvalue safety, we quickly learn to place an extreme value on money and the things it can buy. Instead of placing our trust in God like it says on the currency, we place our trust in the money itself, believing that if we can ever get enough of it, all of our fears will simply vanish.

Now, it's true that a little cash can help. When we have enough to cover a place to live, pay the necessary bills, and meet our basic needs like food and gas for the car, we tend to be less fearful for our safety and well-being. But having "enough" is a mirage and a false promise. It's like a slot machine that pays off with an early win—it convinces you that if you keep playing, you can hit the jackpot. When things are going well and we're bringing in enough money to cover our monthly expenses, with maybe a little extra left over, many of us take a quick measure of our situation and come to the largely unfounded conclusion that we must be pretty good at this financial stuff. Since we can take on the extra monthly payments with no problem, we head down to Better Buys and purchase a faster laptop and a bigger, smarter TV on credit. Soon we find that we "need" a sportier car to impress clients, or we "need" to remodel the kitchen and dining room for entertaining guests. Before long, we find that materialism has become the family's new religion.

Since money quieted some of our fears early on, we now expect it to solve all of our worries. So we give our time, energy, and resources into obtaining as much money as possible and buying as many things as we can, thinking that surrounding ourselves with money and things will make us safer. But it doesn't. Instead, it adds to our fears.

Ask Solomon, one of the wealthiest men who ever lived (after adjusting for inflation). He taught that the more we own, the more we want, and the less satisfied we will be with what we already have (Ecclesiastes 5:10); the more we have, the more we can lose (Ecclesiastes 5:11); and the emptier we feel because we've placed our trust in things, the more we become convinced that we just haven't found the right stuff yet (Ecclesiastes 2:1–17). Like addicts seeking comfort from the very drug that's causing us pain, we look for peace in the things that are adding to our uneasiness. When we don't find the peace we seek in the things we own, out of fear we buy more stuff, which adds to our worries, which causes us to buy more, and so on.

Just as our need for safety convinces us to overvalue money and things, so too our trust in appearances makes materialism our friend. For example, nothing projects strength like material things. From what we drive to who we wear to where we live, every high-end tool and toy is another way to inform others of our prestige and power so they don't dare approach us in a threatening way. So we borrow money that is not ours to present a persona that is not us to prevent others we don't know from becoming a threat to us.

Our obsession with safety and appearances makes our materialism feel perfectly natural. It's the good and sane choice. Fear and greed whisper in our ears, confirming that money and material things are indeed the answer to our problems. Thus fear and greed drive our materialism, making this the most unstable of walls.

The Unstable Home

Volatility in the markets is characterized by huge swings in gains and losses that defy logical explanation. That's how it is in the Home of the Afraid. Our fears lead to emotional instability, erratic thinking, and extreme self-centeredness, and so we turn to material things to boost our sense of well-being, but buying more stuff only leads to more fear. That's why today's homes are so often defined by instability. Behavior isn't predictable, thinking isn't well defined, and decision-making is often haphazard. No one in the home knows what to expect next except for a continued drive to obtain more stuff. Let's take a closer look at these three fear-driven problems.

Emotional Instability

Love is predictable; fear is uncertain. When we are driven by fear, we begin to lose emotional control even as we give our emotions more influence over our lives. Because our fears put us in a vulnerable position, savvy advertisers frequently use an emotional appeal to sell us material things.

We don't really want the truck; we want the feeling of being desired, like the guy in the truck commercial whose girlfriend loves him for his 13,000-pound towing capacity. We don't need the jeans; we need to be noticed like the model wearing the jeans in the magazine ad. We don't feel the need to feed quarters into a slot; we feel the need to be happy and loved like the person in the brochure who just won the jackpot.

Materialism exploits our emotions. And as we allow ourselves to be led by emotions, we become less and less predictable with those emotions. Uncertainty breeds instability, and instability breeds anxiety. Anxiety breeds even greater reliance on material things, because when everything else is changing, we need something physical we can hold on to.

Erratic Thinking

Love isn't always easy, but it is relatively simple. It's not hard to make a good decision when love is the motivation. Fear isn't so evident. When we're being driven by fear, our thinking becomes erratic. We might make a wise choice one minute and a foolish one the next. We might value one thing one day and something different the next. When our motivation is fear, whatever is our greatest fear at the moment dictates our choices. Fear makes for erratic thought patterns and unreliable decision-making.

Extreme Self-Centeredness

Everyone is self-centered to some extent. We emerged from the womb grasping and clutching. As infants, we thought the whole world revolved around us, our wants, and our needs. If our needs weren't met immediately, we communicated our displeasure the only way we knew how—by pitching a fit. It's something we're supposed to grow out of. Based on our daily political and social discourse, however, far too many of us have failed to advance past adolescence and graduate to emotional maturity.

It's time we recognize self-centeredness in ourselves and take steps to eliminate what comedian Brian Regan calls the "me-monster."[4]

Unfortunately, materialism exacerbates the problem. As I make a lifestyle of connecting with things rather than people, I begin to love things and use people instead of loving people and using things. Pretty soon, everything becomes about "me, me, ME!" If others don't agree with this assessment of my primacy, I inform them that they have rudely triggered my fight-flight-or-freeze response (safety), and I click a few buttons online and purchase something flashy (materialism) that will help everyone to see (appearances) just how wonderful I truly am! And all with free two-day delivery! And so the continuous cycle of consumption creates deeper self-centeredness, causing me to want even more.

Volatility—as evidenced by emotional instability, erratic thinking, and extreme self-centeredness—is a by-product of fear. When the home is unstable, you can be sure fear is present there. And where fear is present, materialism is likely one of the ways we're looking for relief.

What Are We Really Buying?

At the heart of materialism is a need for connection. We were created to be in relationship, to connect with others. But fear reminds us there's danger in relationship, in making ourselves vulnerable. Who among us hasn't experienced heartbreak at some point? Many of us have been abused, manipulated, or shamed to varying degrees. We have sought a kind word or helping hand only to find rejection. We needed compassion but received contempt. We've been isolated in moments when we most needed community.

So now, turning to others is frightening. The risk is too great. Yet we still have an innate need for connection, so we turn to material things to fill the need. And the immediate response can be something of a rush. The smell of a new car, the first night in a new house, the feeling of putting on for the first time a suit or dress that looks great and fits perfectly—these can create a palpable sensation that feels like connection. But the thrill of the purchase quickly fades, and we are still alone.

When Jenny and I lived in Birmingham, her job required lots of travel. She enjoyed it; I hated it. I'm glad she got to travel, but I hated the fact that she was gone so much. I was attending graduate school at the time, so I had plenty to do while she was away, but I would still feel incredibly lonely when she left. One weekend when she was out of town, I went to a bookstore to buy a book. I was standing in the checkout line when I suddenly realized how ridiculous it was that I was buying a book. I was in graduate school; I had *stacks* of books I was supposed to be reading. But here I was in a bookstore, buying yet another one. I didn't think much more about it at the time, but I did file it away in my memory.

About six months ago, I was in a bookstore on a Friday afternoon, mainly because it was raining and I couldn't play golf. As I was browsing, I suddenly remembered my thought from years earlier. I stopped and asked myself, *Do you need a book, or are you just bored?* I think it was the latter.

There is nothing wrong with buying a book (especially this book). Reading is a relaxing pastime with many side benefits, including learning something useful, and a bookstore is a great place to go when you're lonely or bored. What interested me on this day was the relationship between my emotions and my money. I was fascinated to wonder—every time I spend a dollar on a book or another item, am I actually spending it on the object itself? Sometimes I'm trying to buy something else.

We see this all the time when people are going through grief. It's not at all unusual for a person to lose a spouse to death and then go on a massive spending spree. Ask an insurance agent about life insurance benefits paid to a surviving spouse. These payouts are generally supposed to last the person for quite a long time, yet the money is often spent in a much shorter time frame. In fact, it's not unusual for a widow to have spent the whole of the life insurance within six months of her husband's death.

Isn't it interesting that we rarely hear about someone working through a midlife crisis by putting a stop to all discretionary spending and completely downsizing? When we think of a midlife crisis, it usually involves someone going on an extreme spending spree, completely changing his or her life by embracing a much more youthful look and lavish lifestyle. Afraid that life is passing them by, such people attempt to purchase things that will turn back the clock and rejuvenate their outlook.

There *is* a direct relationship between how we feel and what we spend. My guess is that every one of us can point back to a purchase we made primarily in hopes of feeling better. Perhaps we didn't think that at the time. We found a way to justify it in the moment, but looking back, we can see that we made the purchase mainly because we were lonely or depressed or just plain bored.

#10 on Your Scorecards but #1 in Your Hearts

Materialism is the belief that money and possessions can meaningfully contribute to our sense of value or worth and satisfaction with life. This is a prevalent belief in modern society despite the complete and utter absence of any proof that it's true. On the contrary, study after study has shown that people who are materialistic are more prone to compulsive spending and running up debt while putting aside very little in the way of savings. Materialistic people are also much more likely to experience significant struggles with anxiety and depression as well as strained relationships.

Science tells us that materialism doesn't make life better.

The Bible told us the same thing long ago.

To "covet" something is to excessively dwell on a wrong desire; it's an erotic term applied to material things. The words *covet* and *Cupid* are related, having the same Latin roots that conjure images of passions boiling over.[5] In the same way that a young man might have such lustful feelings toward a woman that he might make poor decisions, so too we can let our desires get the better of us and make poor decisions in pursuing things that are not ours.

It's such an issue for humanity that God tried to protect us from it, listing it among the Ten Commandments. The tenth commandment warns us against desiring what rightfully belongs to our neighbor—his house, his wife, his servants, his animals, or anything else (Exodus 20:17). Upon first reading, it's unclear why a prohibition against coveting would get equal time with restrictions against murder, theft, idolatry, or even giving false testimony in court. Yet the seriousness of these other commands makes it clear how dangerous God considers the sin of coveting.

Notice that this commandment differs from the other nine.[6] Murder, theft, adultery, even taking the Lord's name in vain—those are physical acts. But coveting is primarily a matter of the heart. We can't usually look at a person and tell if he is coveting or not. So this commandment completes the Big Ten by showing us that God desires not just the right action but also the right attitude.

According to Matthew 22:36–40, all the teachings of the Law and the prophets can be summed up in two commands:

> 1. Love God with all your heart, your soul, and your mind.
> 2. Love your neighbor as yourself.

One reason coveting rates such a prominent mention in the Law is that it's a deadly heart condition that can weaken our resistance to so many other kinds of sin such as idolatry, greed, envy, pride, adultery, and theft, just to name a few. As a matter of fact, covetousness positions us to be in direct violation of what the Lord identifies as His two greatest commandments. For how can I love God with all my mind and all my heart if my thoughts and affections keep returning to the idea of possessing something He has given to another? How can I love my neighbor when I'm more interested in what he owns than in who he is?

Coveting is wrong because it means that our eyes are locked on what those around us possess—what they have, how they got it, and how we can get it. That's one of the real problems with materialism: it offers a counterfeit connection. We need others because that's the way God made us. But connecting with others on a personal level is dangerous and full of risks. So fear drives us to keep our relationships on a surface level, based on little more than mutual interests, shared geography, and perhaps a few material things others have that we might be able to borrow sometime.

> That's one of the real problems
>
> with materialism: it offers a
>
> counterfeit connection.

Once again, we've turned to material things in hopes that we won't be alone but we will be safe. Yet with material things, we are neither.

We're Infecting Kids with a Terrible Disease

I'm a bit of a germaphobe, although I'm what I call an "ignorant germaphobe." I'll shake several hundred hands before and after services while occasionally touching my nose, mouth, and eyes. When I get home, I sit down to eat, never remembering to wash my hands until the next time I use the restroom.

But if I find out that someone I know has a bug, I freak out. If one of my coworkers calls in sick with the common cold, my throat will automatically start hurting. If you call me tomorrow and mention having had a stomach virus overnight, and I'm able to re-create some scenario—*any* scenario—in which you and I could have touched the same thing, I'll start feeling sick. Of course, if I am unaware of an illness going around, I don't worry about it. But if I learn that somebody somewhere in the Western Hemisphere is sick and possibly contagious, I obsess over it.

When it comes to materialism, we should remember that we are dealing with a highly infectious disease. It spreads invisibly and aggressively like a snotty nose at a day-care facility. Every single day, each of us is exposed to this disease, and no one is immune. Not only do we need to exercise preventative measures to reduce our exposure to this menace, but we must also take steps to stop the spread of the germs that have already attached themselves to us.

In the bestselling book *The Millionaire Next Door*, the authors write that a significant mistake many people make while trying to build wealth is that they move into too big of a house in too nice of a neighborhood. The problem isn't the house, which might be a good investment. The problem is that in the nice neighborhood, the neighbors will have nicer cars, greener lawns, better furniture, etc. Without even believing in the tenth commandment, the authors of this book warn against surrounding ourselves with lavish things because they know human nature.[7]

Who of us would ever give our kids something we knew they would become addicted to and would ruin their lives? How would we judge a parent who got his child hooked on meth at a young age? How do we view a woman who takes illicit drugs when she's pregnant and eventually gives birth to the child with drugs in the baby's system? And yet we are teaching our kids that things matter, that life is better when you have more, and that they should do everything in their power to make a lot of money so they can buy the stuff they need to have the life they want. We're hooking our kids on materialism before they are old enough to decide for themselves. By the time they have the mental capacity to understand the problem, most of them are already too dependent on material things to easily detoxify from their addiction.

Do you tell your kids that money and possessions don't matter when your primary means of showing them love is to buy them stuff?

If you're a grandma or grandpa, are you more interested in being the "fun" grandparent than in helping the parents to train up a heart that doesn't covet the things of others?

Can't Buy Me Love

The real problem with materialism is that, however much you spend, you can't buy what's important. Even the credit card companies, which usually promise the moon, admit that "there are some things money can't buy."[8]

Yet instead of putting in the effort—and risking pain—to build lasting, loving relationships with friends, family, and our significant others, we treat our relationships as simple transactions we make to reduce and/or hide our fears. People then become one more material thing we purchase in an attempt to buy happiness. And when they don't deliver, they are thrown away and replaced. Priceless.

As we've seen, love values people and uses things, while fear values things and uses people. Although fear alters how we view people, it doesn't change how we were created, which is to need other people. But fear causes us to push others away and put up walls around us, thus creating further isolation, sorrow, and loneliness and increasing our worries. Woe to us when we fall and have no one there to help us up (Ecclesiastes 4:10)!

> Love values people and uses things, while
>
> fear values things and uses people.

Social media might be the best example of how we try to meet our longing for connection with idolatry of material things. We now seek to replace real-life relationships with pseudo-connections on various online platforms. These online relationships often feel real, but a thousand likes or comments can't replace a shoulder to cry on when life is tough. A million followers are of less value than one true friend who mows your yard when you are in the hospital giving birth to your first child.

Yes, we can interact with others on social media, but we can't truly connect—not to the depths that we were created to do so with one another. But social media is safer. It removes some of the fears of rejection or risk of embarrassment that comes with real relationships. That's why fear tells me to text when love tells me I should call when tension arises in a relationship.

Let's say I've done something wrong, or at least had my intentions misinterpreted. Love compels me to call the other person and talk it through, to make sure the relationship is healthy. But a call feels dangerous. What if the person doesn't answer? What if he is angry? Sending a text is easier, less risky. A text won't force the other person to choose to respond or not respond right away. Texting avoids any nervousness in my voice if I call, and it keeps me from being put on the spot if the person asks a difficult question. This way, I'll have time to calculate my response. Texting slows down the back-and-forth and allows me to opt out of the conversation under the guise that I got busy or had to take a call. If I call the person, I won't have that luxury. Once a phone conversation starts, there is no easy way out.

Love says to call. Fear says to text. So I text. I use the material things at hand to maintain my tenuous connection with another, a connection that feels safer than a real person-to-person relationship. Of course, this approach doesn't lessen my fear. Instead, my fear increases.

Jesus or Madonna?

In 1985, when "Material Girl" hit the *Billboard* charts, music critics weren't overly kind. Most dismissed the song as the cynical anthem of the modern world, although a few hailed it as an insightful satirical critique of the contemporary materialistic culture. In any case, the message was clear: we live in a world that believes money and material things can bring us contentment, satisfaction, and meaning.

Two thousand years ago, Jesus came to this planet as God's ultimate declaration to the world. He came that we might have life and have it more abundantly (John 10:10). Madonna and Jesus both claimed to point to a way in which we might experience abundant life. Only one of these ways can be right.

Life experience tells us that money and possessions have never produced the happiness they promised. But rather than learning the lesson and trying a different way, we continue to double and triple down on the hope of finding meaning through material goods. While we might say that we know Jesus is right, we keep living as though Madonna knows best.

We are ruled by fear, and we continually turn to materialistic things in hopes that our fears will be diminished. The result is that we experience even more fear, chaos, and volatility. We long for a better way, but we don't know how to live differently from what has been modeled for us by our parents, our neighbors, and the culture we live in.

Think on These Things

1. If volatility is a sign of fear, how fearful is your home? Is your family emotionally predictable?

2. Think of an item you purchased that you really didn't need. What were you *really* buying at the time? What emotional need were you trying to fill with your purchase?

3. What are you teaching your kids by the way you handle money? Do you often buy nonessential items using credit cards? Do you tend to spend more than you make each month? Do you give gifts instead of verbally expressing your love?

4. What are some practical steps you can take right now to inoculate your family against the disease of materialism? If they already have the disease, how can you fight its spread while working toward a cure?

Chapter 5

Power: The Path to Paranoia

There is a time when a man lords it over others to his own hurt.

Ecclesiastes 8:9 NIV

For even the Son of Man came not to be served but to serve, and to give his life as a ransom for many.

Mark 10:45

Holiday planning was easy at first for Chris and Mackenzie. With his family living in California and her family back in Iowa, they decided to rotate Thanksgiving and Christmas every year. One year they would celebrate Thanksgiving with Chris's family, then Christmas with Mackenzie's; the next year the order was switched. Neither set of parents got all the holiday time they wanted, but the system seemed equitable and it worked.

But Mackenzie knew this plan couldn't last. When their first son, Julian, was an infant, it didn't matter where he woke up on Christmas Day, but as he grew older, Mackenzie wanted him to experience Christmas morning at their Colorado home. Early on, she told Chris that the day would quickly come when the holiday plan would need to be renegotiated. When baby Jack was born, Mackenzie decided she would do two more years of rotation, but then things would change. When her kids were old enough to remember the holidays, they were going to wake up in their own beds at their own house Christmas morning.

Two more years of Thanksgivings and Christmases came and went. Mackenzie knew her parents would be disappointed by the change, but they would understand. She had already had several conversations with them over the years to help soften the blow when the day came. And they were, in fact, supportive.

Chris hadn't been so courageous. While he was on the same page as his wife, he had tried to avoid this conversation with his parents for as long as possible. Not that his dad would care; his dad never cared. Chris's father had learned long ago to remain quiet and go along with whatever his wife, Kathy, desired. Kathy was energetic and driven and successful at everything she did. Even as she was taking care of her elderly mother, she managed to be an amazing long-distance grandmother. Kathy loved Mackenzie, but Mackenzie was always a bit intimidated by her mother-in-law. She often felt that Kathy second-guessed her parenting decisions. While she had been welcomed into Chris's family, she also felt as though she were blamed for the fact that his family couldn't always come together for big occasions as they once did.

As spring turned to summer, Mackenzie reminded Chris more than once that he needed to tell his mom that the holiday rotation was changing that year. Thanksgiving would continue to rotate between the two families, but Christmas would be spent at home.

Either or both families were welcome to join them, but Chris and Mackenzie and the kids would not be joining the families in their Christmas traditions. When summer turned to fall, Chris still had not made the call to his mother. It would have been a hard discussion no matter what, but it was complicated by the fact that this was the year they would normally spend Christmas at his parents' house in California. His parents would be the first to experience their absence because of the decision Chris and Mackenzie had made.

Consider how this discussion *should* go. Chris should be able to call his mother and explain the situation. The rotation had worked for several years, but the kids were getting older. Both he and Mackenzie loved their families, but they also wanted their kids to grow up with the kind of memories they had of waking up in *their* beds on Christmas morning, running down *their* stairs, and opening the presents under *their* tree. Kathy would have every right to be disappointed and sad, but she should also understand. She had the same feelings when *her* children were young, being torn between wanting to be faithful to family traditions while also forming new traditions as a new family. She should encourage Chris to spend Christmas however he wants. Kathy should be flexible to look for new ways they could spend time together and feel gratitude for all the Christmas memories they had made. She should then reassure Mackenzie, too, that they were making the right decision.

But how do you think the discussion went? Chris refused to make the call. Finally, Mackenzie dialed the number and forced the phone into his hand. Kathy was not pleased. She didn't listen and support the young couple. Instead, she interrupted, questioned, and guilted her son. Mackenzie was being selfish in Kathy's eyes. Kathy's mom was getting older, and Chris knew better than to skip this Christmas. What if this were her mother's last one?

If you were to ask Kathy, she would say the issue at play regarding Christmas is that of love. If her son and daughter-in-law make the loving choice, they will spend Christmas with her at her house. Kathy will get to see her grandkids, and all the kids will get to see Kathy's mother. But the real issue at play is *power*. Afraid of what might happen if traditions change, Kathy has turned to the idol of power, hoping not to experience those fears. In her mind, life will be simpler and better for everybody if she is in charge. As long as her son does what she thinks is best, everything will work out fine. But if Chris and Mackenzie choose their own course, there's no telling just how bad Christmas might be.

When we are afraid, we do not naturally respond in love. Instead, we often try a power play. Even with the people we love the most, we don't take a step back, honor their personhood, and allow them to make the best decision they can. Instead, we coerce, manipulate, and guilt, all in an attempt to get our way. We don't think of it as power. To us, it feels like love. We're merely trying to get others to do what is best for everyone. But in reality, our actions are not loving. They are manipulative acts born of fear.

The Problem with Power

Power can be a good thing. A pastor can use social influence to help others. A country can use military force to free an oppressed people. A bank can use its monetary power to enable a start-up company to get off the ground. When power is motivated by love and used to serve others, it can be a force for good.

But when power is driven by fear rather than love, the results are often catastrophic. Rather than a pastor helping others, he can use his power and influence to spiritually abuse people. The same country that uses its military power to liberate others can also use it to oppress its own citizens. Money that can be a catalyst for good can also be used to bribe government officials or manipulate stock prices.

Power driven by love is self-sacrificing; in love, we use power to serve others. Power driven by fear is self-serving; out of fear, we end up using people for our benefit. When fear guides our agendas, we turn people into objects that we use to get what we desire. Rather than exhausting ourselves to serve others, we exhaust others so they can serve us.

Even at home.

Power is the perfect final wall to the Home of the Afraid.

Few things offer us the facade of security like power. From an early age, nearly all of us experience abuse from one or more persons who have power over us. It might have been a short-tempered parent or an older sibling who used you like an emotional and/or physical punching bag. Perhaps there was a teacher who, having control over little in her own life, liked to control kids. We continue to see it in adulthood—middle managers whose only joy is lording their power over us, lawyers who write the rules for themselves, politicians who seek power to feed their egos, pastors who prefer to be served rather than serve. Surrounded by real-life examples such as these, we have been trained to grasp for power for ourselves. Not to have the power is to put ourselves at risk. Thus our need for safety encourages us to seek power.

Appearances do much the same thing. Having power gives the impression of strength. Power scares some people away, causes some to submit to us, and encourages others to serve us on the assumption that our influence might benefit them. When we show strength, we aren't questioned, doubted, or debated. Power is appearance's great friend. If we have control, we have the appearance of strength. If we can't have actual power, we can project power in hopes of lessening our fears.

The connection between appearances and power is why fame is so valued in our culture. Celebrity looks like it is something when in reality it's not. It masquerades as importance but without any real consequence. Fame by itself requires no expertise, no ability, and no substance. Yet it can feel like all of those things. Why does the endorsement of a celebrity drive sales more than words spoken by an expert? Why do we turn to the Twitter accounts of famous people for their reflections on a current news story? Fame feels influential, but it's all smoke and mirrors with little actual value.

Our thirst for safety and appearance leads us up to lean on the walls of power and materialism. These two walls complement each other. In our culture, money is power and power is money. As we idolize one, our desire for the other grows.

> In our culture, money is power and power is money. As we idolize one, our desire for the other grows.

Unhealthy By-products of Fear

When we grasp for power out of fear, power often masks itself as love. We deceive ourselves into thinking that our way is the right way for others and ourselves, and as long as we're in control, things will turn out for the best. But if we cede control, we are all in trouble. All of this leads to some unhealthy behaviors.

Manipulation. The best tool for manipulating another person is guilt. If Grandma doesn't get her way regarding where you spend Christmas, she will guilt you into believing that to wake up Christmas Day in your own bed is an unloving gesture toward her. She will bring up all the times she sacrificed for you, expecting that you will now do the same for her, even if it means your young kids never experience a Christmas morning at home.

Attack. Rather than sticking with the issue at hand in a disagreement, we may attack the character or personhood of the other person in an attempt to gain control of the disagreement. If we can dehumanize the other, we won't have to deal with his or her ideas or opinions, and we won't be vulnerable. Attacking is a way to put the spotlight on the other person so it won't be on us.

Demands. These are different from boundaries. We have every right to define what we are and are not willing to do. Making demands, however, is an attempt to define what others should or should not do. We discredit the decision-making of the other person and attempt to force him or her to do things our way.

Victimhood. Sometimes overlooked, playing the role of victim has gained popularity as a power play in today's culture. To be able to claim that your feelings were hurt puts you in the position of victim. From this position, you get to dictate the worth of the other person and determine how both parties will move forward. While legitimate victimhood is an important issue, *pretending* to be a victim is a mask for seeking power. Many husbands and wives pout to gain power, not because they are genuinely hurt by what their spouses have done.

Screaming and Silence. These are often two sides of the same coin. The spouse who yells and the one who gives the silent treatment take two different tacks to reach the same outcome: they want to avoid an honest conversation. The screamer does it with force, shouting to scare away the other person, like a barking dog trying to intimidate a potential threat so that it goes away. The spouse who ignores a conversation or gives the silent treatment (a.k.a., the cold shoulder) seeks the same outcome: he or she wants to avoid dealing with the issue at hand. Rather than yelling, the silent spouse emotionally shuts down.

Power Struggles with Our Children

In *Happily: 8 Commitments of Couples Who Laugh, Love, and Last*, I wrote about avoiding power struggles in marriage.[1] In any circumstance where people are in a relationship—marriage, parenting, friendships, coworkers, etc.—there is a temptation to enter into a power struggle. Our intentions are good. We desire to have power in the relationship so things go the way we want. We believe it will be for the benefit of all involved. But what we fail to see is how a struggle for power creates chaos.

In many ways, the frustration between parents and teenagers is the by-product of a power struggle. As children grow, they begin to desire (and take) more control of their lives. Often, they want the *benefits* of freedom before they are ready to handle the *responsibilities* of freedom. They want power, but their parents understand that the kids aren't ready yet.

In some instances, the parents can't cede control to their growing children even when the children deserve it. Both parties grow frustrated as the struggle intensifies. I sometimes describe the teenage years as "ripping apart." Parents and kids may be tightly bonded, but as the kids grow and leave the house, the transition is often not a smooth one. In many cases, a tearing away is taking place. While this transition is a bit of a struggle in any family, the struggle is much greater when fear rules the home. Anytime we are driven by fear, giving power to another can be overwhelming. So we attempt to hold on to it with everything we have.

Power and Worth

One reason we love power is that it's the ultimate way to hide. Teachers don't have to answer questions from their students. Suspects don't interrogate police officers. Judges aren't called on the carpet by juries. Parents don't have to explain themselves to children. Whoever is in power can question without being questioned, hold accountable without being held accountable, punish without being punished, and force others to follow the rules without following the rules themselves. Is it any wonder why we desire power? When we have it, we can project strength and righteousness without ever being tested. We can use our position of power to hold others down without ever having to prove ourselves.

But ultimately, we want power because we have believed the lie: *I am somebody if I'm more powerful than you.* We define an individual's worth by the power he or she wields. So the general is of more value than his soldiers. The employer is of more importance than her employees. When I have more power than you, I am more of a person than you. This is why oppressed people are so often quick to oppress others once they come to power. We would like to think that having experienced oppression, they would never do to others what has been done to them. Yet the long history of humanity shows that when oppressed people come to power, they oppress others. It's because we believe the lie that power equals a person's worth.

A Stark Contrast

The plot of the human story was set when our first parents disobeyed God and ate of the forbidden fruit. The sales pitch that convinced them to disobey went like this: "For God knows that when you eat of it your eyes will be opened, and you will be like God, knowing good and evil" (Genesis 3:5). I can almost guarantee that Adam and Eve didn't hear a word after "like God"—just as we don't understand the caveats of the auto loan once we've decided we can make the monthly payment on that shiny new truck. Or we don't read the fine print when booking a great vacation. It's easy for us to be shocked at the actions of our first parents, but at least they sold their souls for something as lofty as being like God. These days we tend to betray ourselves and others for far less.

The tempter spoke to the core desire of humanity. We want power. Any position other than the first position promises danger. We don't want to submit to anyone. We don't want to follow another. We refuse to be told what to do. We want the power so we can do as we wish, not have to change, and be free from all restraints. If we're in charge, everyone else will have to do things our way.

Now, contrast humanity's grasping at the possibility of power with what Paul wrote about Jesus: "who, though he was in the form of God, did not count equality with God a thing to be grasped, but emptied himself, by taking the form of a servant" (Philippians 2:6–7). Jesus, who rightfully had the power, willfully let it go. It wasn't something He had to hold tightly. Instead, He was willing to let go of all the trappings of the Godhead to accomplish the plan of the Father. Whereas humanity sacrificed obedience in exchange for the promise of power, Jesus gave up the adoration of power to maintain His position as an obedient Son. The contrast couldn't be starker.

Power is not a bad thing until we chase after it or use it with wrong motives. The Bible has a plethora of examples in which God gave strength to individuals with the intent that they use their position to benefit others. We aren't expected to avoid power in the same way that we are supposed to stay away from coveting, lying, stealing, and other sins. But although power can be used for good, it comes with significant risks and temptations. Certainly we should never grasp after power at the expense of obedience.

When power is entrusted to you and used for the well-being of others, it is good. Liberation occurs. The voiceless are given a platform. Injustices are reversed. When power is sought after for the worship of self, it is an idol. Power makes an excellent tool but a terrible god.

> Power makes an excellent
> tool but a terrible god.

The difficulty is that we are easily deceived, readily corrupted. We convince ourselves that we are grasping at power for some noble cause when, in fact, we are doing it out of fear or greed. Either we want all the trappings that come with power, or we're afraid of what might happen if we are not in charge. In either case, having the power is all about "me, me, ME!" again, and everyone else is either an opponent in our fight for control or a mere bystander in our pursuit of power.

That's no way to lead a nation or a family.

Love Instead of Power

In too many homes, power is destroying any chance at intimacy, because no one wants to be vulnerable when their vulnerability might be abused. The better approach is love. Love submits rather than overpowers.

In Ephesians 5:21, Paul instructed the church that we are to submit to one another out of reverence for Jesus. This admonition comes at the end of a passage about how brothers and sisters in Christ ought to worship together, and the same holds true for how we ought to interact with one another at home.

Love tells us to submit to one another by treating everyone with kindness and respect, by putting each other's needs ahead of our own, and by restraining our bad behaviors and instead doing what is right. If you want the rest of the family to look up to you, if you want to be great in their eyes and in God's eyes, you must determine to be a servant to all (Mark 10:43).

When we choose love, we drop the power plays. We refuse to manipulate, coerce, yell, or go silent. We reject the role of victim and actively seek to love. When we reject power, trust can be built in its stead. When I know my spouse isn't out to get me, I can trust her to be there for me. When children know their parents will be consistent, they don't always have to flinch when they do something wrong. When families know they can work together, real communication becomes possible.

Whereas power produces paranoia, love produces peace. Kindness pervades the home. Difficult conversations have a characteristic of gentleness. Yes, there will be struggles, and tough days will happen now and then. But when love rules the home, no one has to be afraid because everyone knows the family can and will endure. When love defines our home, the arrows are pointed outward and we fight together against the external threats.

It's Time to Topple the Home of the Afraid

The Home of the Afraid is not constructed with great foresight or intentions. Experts aren't consulted. Time and energy are not spent to select just the right materials. Instead, we make choices based on fear, and we turn to the things that feel natural in a fallen world.

Society promises shelter, and so we seek relief in valuing safety above all things. In hopes of being safe, we promote appearances even if those appearances don't fully represent the truth of who we are. Materialism and power have given us moments of rest in a wearisome world, so we assume that having more things and better things will provide us with a better life, along with greater strength and power.

Safety, appearances, materialism, and power are not concepts that we daily decide will dictate the direction of our lives. Instead, they subtly express themselves in every small decision we make. As fear rules us, it drives us toward these things. Sadly, they do not alleviate our concerns. While they can't keep fear out of our homes, they do an excellent job of trapping it inside the walls.

Yet rather than recognizing that our way isn't working, we continue to double down and seek more power, more things, better appearances, and a greater allegiance to safety. And so our fear continues to grow.

Thankfully there is a better way.

It's time to topple the Home of the Afraid.

Think on These Things

1. What role does guilt or manipulation play in your family? How is using either of these a power play?

2. Are you more likely to scream during an argument or give your spouse the silent treatment? What are you hoping to accomplish with this approach?

3. Identify what kind of power you hold within your family. How would Jesus change the way you view and use that power?

4. Of the four fear-driven dynamics we've discussed—safety, appearances, materialism, and power—which are evident in your home? How do they make their presence felt?

Part II

The Home of the Brave

Chapter 6

Love: The Antidote to Fear

Therefore be imitators of God, as beloved children. And walk in love, as Christ loved us and gave himself up for us, a fragrant offering and sacrifice to God.

Ephesians 5:1–2

There is no fear in love, but perfect love casts out fear.

1 John 4:18

The spotlight shines on the young woman perched high above the crowd. With a breathtaking leap, she soars through the air, clinging to a bar held aloft by nothing more than a pair of ropes. She swings back and forth gracefully but powerfully, building momentum. At the same time, across the way, her partner begins a rhythmic swinging of his own while hanging upside down by his knees. At just the right moment, the young woman lets go of the bar, somersaults through the air, and is caught by her partner.

The flying trapeze is a mixture of acrobatics, gymnastics, and extreme trust. It is an act of fantastic artistry that pushes human beings to their physical and mental limits. At its riskiest, the trapeze act is performed without a harness or net, meaning the artists are placing their very lives in the hands of each other. However, trapeze skills are never learned in that way. They are first attempted low to the ground and always with a safety net. Only when skills are refined and mastered is the net removed and the act performed at full height in the big top.

While the act is dangerous, trapeze artists lower the risk as much as possible by learning their routines in a safe environment. Without a safety net, performers could never develop their skills, try new things, or advance in their artistry. The net empowers growth, risk, and adventure.

Life comes with many of the same demands as the flying trapeze. It requires risk, adventure, skill, trust, and dependency on others. We can't just stand on our platforms and experience all we were meant to be and do. We must embrace the spotlight, leap from our safe perches, swing with all our might to build momentum, and then let go of the bar—all while trusting that others will do their jobs with practiced skill and catch us before we fall.

Courage is demanded from us in this life, but learning and honing life skills requires more than sheer bravery. The secret is the net. Its presence empowers us to try new things, perfect our techniques, and test our limits. Meanwhile, the net ensures our safety, which allows us to improve our skills with lesser risk of injury.

When it comes to life, love is our safety net. It promises to keep us from hitting the ground even if our talent slips or our timing is off. As long as the net is secured below us, we know we have the freedom to try, learn, experiment, and even fail. While we hope for success, the net doesn't demand we succeed every time.

Yes, we live in a world that requires courage, but courage is merely a by-product of something greater. Brave people aren't stronger than the rest of us; they have safety nets that they can trust. They can demonstrate great courage because they know that if all else fails, their net of love will catch them.

So this is my task as a husband, father, and friend. My challenge is to love others so they will feel safe to risk, attempt, learn, try, fail, and try again. They don't need my directions or commands nearly as much as they need my love. They don't need my opinions or teachings half as much as they need to know that I am there, loving and supporting them. When they are secure in that love, they are free to push away from the platform and swing. They can twirl and flip. They can let go of the bar, hoping they will be caught but knowing that even if everything goes wrong, I will still be there.

When I am not courageous, it's not a sign that I'm a coward so much as an indication that I'm failing to embrace love. When those I care about fail to take a risk or grow, it doesn't mean I should question their courage or push them to act bravely. It means I should make them more confident in my love for them. We all have the capacity for courage *if* we are sure there's a net waiting to catch us should we fall.

Husbands, love your wives in such a way that they are willing to stretch themselves toward becoming who God made them to be.

Wives, love your husbands so they can risk—in godly ways—vulnerability.

Parents, love your children so they can venture from home with the security of knowing they always have a place where they can return.

Teachers, love your students so they can be brave enough to process new information and consider new ideas.

Friends, love each other in hopes that you both will have the fortitude to explore uncharted territories.

Employers, love your employees so they can have the courage to become the best they can be at what they do.

Remember that love is defined by much more than how you feel about the other person. Love is a choice that expresses itself in an action. In fact, we must make the choice anew every day to love the other person through our actions.

Without love, life is too risky. We have to play it safe and stick with what we know. But when love is present and persistent, we are free to experiment, attempt, fail, and succeed. We are empowered to reach out and love others.

Life demands courage.

Love is the net that enables courage to grow.

Learning to Love

My grandmother was one of the most servant-oriented people I've ever met. It wasn't until very late in her life that I saw her sit down and not be at work doing something—sewing a dress, fixing a pie, cleaning the kitchen, preparing for the next day's activities. I've long said that my grandfather taught me tenderness and my grandmother taught me toughness. Born in 1922, my grandmother had a childhood that created within her a fierce love for her family and a firm approach to work. If everyone served like she did, the world would never be in want.

At the age of ninety, my grandmother developed cancer. She was shocked her life was coming to an end. But her astonishment was borderline amusing. Having lived well past the average life expectancy, she was not yet ready to go. Because her father lived well into his nineties, my Mammaw was always convinced she would make it to a hundred. She knew it wouldn't be easy, but there was never a doubt in her mind. So when she received the cancer diagnosis, she felt cheated out of ten years of her life.

Days before she moved to hospice, it was just the two of us in her room one afternoon. "This is so hard, Kevin," she said.

"I know, but they are going to do everything in their power to make you comfortable," I replied.

Her brow furrowed. "Dying isn't hard. It's hard to lay here while other people wait on me."

For as long as my Mammaw could remember, she had been the servant. She was the one who made sure her daddy had supper on the table. She was the one who made clothes for my mom and uncle. She was the one who sacrificed everything when my grandfather's health was failing. Now, in the final days of her life, she was well loved and cared for by nurses, doctors, families, and friends. And she hated it. For my Mammaw, it was easy to love, but it wasn't always easy to *be* loved.

Being loved should come to us naturally, right? After all, no one has to be taught to accept love from a mother or grandmother. It's pretty easy to receive a hug from a loving parent or to sit down for a home-cooked meal at Grandma's house. And so most of us assume that we know how to be loved.

We don't.

We have no problem being liked, but we struggle to be loved. This struggle can express itself in a variety of ways—keeping people at a distance, downplaying compliments, not believing others when they say they love us, refusing to be waited on by a friend or family member when we're sick or injured, and so forth. Yet somehow, very few of us are aware that we have difficulty in this area. Love is in such short supply in this world that none of us can imagine rejecting it when it's offered. But we do.

Recognizing our struggle to accept love leads us to a second revelation: we struggle to *give* love too. We like to think we know how to love, that it comes easily to "mostly good" people such as ourselves. And when we feel love, it often seems easy to act in the way we should toward the object of our affection. But as those feelings fade, as feelings are wont to do, it's not always so easy to act in a loving way.

That's because love does *not* come naturally to those who live in a fallen world. From the time Adam and Eve ate of the forbidden fruit, it has been human nature for people to put themselves first. Our preset mode is to act in our own best interest without worrying much about how our choices will affect others. This is a problem because real love is all about placing the needs of someone else before your own. Love is the opposite of selfishness, whereas fear drives us to prioritize our own needs and wants.

> ## Love does *not* come naturally to those who live in a fallen world.

Love and fear are the only two choices in this equation. There is no third option. Either we will consciously choose the way of love, or we will be ruled by fear. Tragically, many families, friends, coworkers, and communities never recognize the choice that is before them, and so they fail to understand the daily need to intentionally demonstrate love in their attitudes and actions. In part, this is because the common assumption in a humanistic society is that (1) people are basically good and (2) good people will choose to love. Assuming love, they rarely get it—or give it.

This is sadly true even in churches. In church, we sing about love and preach about building our lives and homes around the teachings of the One who told us to "fear not" and "love one another." Yet even churches can be driven by fear. Too many churches make choices based on what it takes to keep key contributors rather than reach new people. Too many are afraid of taking risks, so they play it safe. Too many worry more about the appearance of being right than actually serving others. And too many are as characterized by materialism and a thirst for power as any secular organization in their communities. Ask them, and they will tell you about the importance of love; examine them, and you will see a group of people ruled by fear.

God did not put us here to collect the most toys, protect our positions, put on a good show for our fellow man, or hide ourselves within the safety of our homes and churches. He put us here to love others as He has loved us (John 15:12). Because love does not come naturally to human beings, He is changing those who follow Christ to be more like Him—to think, act, and love more like Jesus did (Romans 8:29; 2 Corinthians 3:18). Thus, following Christ is about learning to love.

The Home of the Brave is ruled by one abiding principle:

We are learning how to love and how to be loved.

What many people take for granted, residents of the Home of the Brave pursue with great intentionality. Whereas the Home of the Afraid is about hiding fear, trying to minimize fear, and longing to be feared, the Home of the Brave is a training ground for learning to love and be loved.

God intended for the family to be the place where we first learn to love, share, and work together. The home is where we are meant to care for one another, support one another, keep each other safe, and put each other's needs ahead of our own. It's where children are to be nurtured, instructed, and given the knowledge and tools to love God and love their neighbors (including those neighbors who share their room, cook their dinner, and make them brush their teeth before bed).

Isn't it time we embrace God's design for the family and tear down these ramshackle homes that have been corroded by fear and poorly subdivided by the emotional walls between us? Isn't it time we build something different? Something better? I'm not saying it will be easy. Love is never the natural or easy way of doing things. And you can be sure we will meet resistance and experience a few failures when attempting to do something that's so foreign to our nature and to this culture.

What Love Truly Looks Like

Sadly, most of the world has no idea what love really is. Songs, movies, TV shows, novels, self-help books, podcasts, and other forms of popular culture generate billions of dollars every year telling us that love is a kind of force, a powerful emotion that overwhelms our senses until it expresses itself to its object by way of an action, usually a heartfelt gesture. If this were the case, love would be out of our control. If the force isn't with us, if we're not *feeling* it, we can hardly be expected to love. We can't help how we feel, can we? Of course we can.

Despite what the world tells us, love is not a force. It's not something we fall in and out of like slipping on a cosmic banana peel. Although love can generate intense feelings, it is much more than an emotion. Love is a *choice*, a way of behaving. It is a choice that expresses itself in an *action*. Feeling may or may not be part of it. When Jesus told His disciples to love one another (John 13:34), He wasn't saying, "Have a continual feeling of affection toward each other"; He was commanding them to act in a loving way toward one another.

Far too often, actions we think of as love are something else entirely. In many cases, for example, we mistake fear for love. We think it is love that keeps us from being direct with a friend when something difficult needs to be said; in reality, it's the fear of rejection. We think it is love that motivates us to shield our children from the natural consequences of their poor choices; in fact, it's the fear of being a bad parent. We think it's love when we mask our emotions and pretend that everything is fine, but it's not; it's the fear of making ourselves vulnerable.

> Far too often, actions we think of as
> love are something else entirely.

Consider the phrase "God is love" (1 John 4:8). These three words are from one of the most straightforward and beautiful verses in the Bible. But if we fail to understand the nature of love, this verse may leave us with a gross misunderstanding of God's character. So how can we comprehend the true nature of love? In order to know what love really looks like, we must have it shown to us.

This is what Jesus did. He defined love for us by how He lived and how He died. Yet despite the fact that mankind has been reading the four gospels for two thousand years, we have some pretty strange ideas about love. For us, love is often characterized by blind acceptance, good feelings, and the absence of tension in a relationship. But for God, love has none of those qualities.

While God's love may involve blanket acceptance—He loves you no matter what you have done—it is not blind acceptance. He knows you better than you know yourself. And while He loves you despite your sins, His love changes who you are.

While God's love may give us good feelings, His love can convict us of our sins, cause us deep regret, and give us a longing to change who we are. His idea of love can make us highly uncomfortable.

While God's love may bring peace, it does not always relieve the tension in our lives. In fact, His love may insist that we face some difficult truths and confront some very awkward aspects of our relationships.

If we accept as true that God declared Himself to be love and that His definition of love is fully exemplified in the life of Christ, then we need to recognize and accept that everything Jesus did in the Gospels defined for us what real love looks like. For instance, it was real love that

- rebuked the Pharisees,
- told the adulterous woman to sin no more,
- warned His followers that they would be hated,
- spoke about the horrors of hell, and
- drove money changers and merchants out of the house of God.

These actions, which revealed the love of Jesus, bear little resemblance to our modern-day conceptions of love.

Usually when I hear the phrase "God is love" in today's culture, the word "but" precedes it. One person proposes a thought or action, and the other objects by saying, "But God is love." A better way to handle this situation is when someone proposes a thought or action in the name of God, we can ask, "Is that loving?" It's a question we should be asking every day.

Is it loving to say nothing to a friend who's making a horrific decision because "I've got to follow my heart"? Probably not.

Is it loving to stand on a street corner, yelling at complete strangers that their actions are sinful and they're headed for hell? Clearly not.

Sometimes love calls out sin but at other times does not.

Sometimes love yells but at other times is silent.

Sometimes love is stern and strict but at other times is soft.

Love is far more complicated than we often believe, and many of our clichés, song lyrics, and snap judgments regarding its nature are drastically wrong.

God has revealed Himself as love, and Jesus showed us what the true nature of love is (John 15:13). To assume knowledge is often arrogant and sometimes dangerous, but to ignore God's revelation is always foolish. The wise course is for us to seek understanding regarding the true nature of love through prayer and the study of His Word.

"God is love" doesn't mean what you or I think. It means what God thinks. The family that lives in the Home of the Brave recognizes this, and its members humble themselves to pursue the meaning of love so that they can live by the way of love.

Love Is Returned

Those of us who occupy the Home of the Brave know that we need to have love defined for us. We need to see it in action, to attempt to understand it, and to learn its ways and practice them. Only then can we uncover the lies we have believed about love and begin to write a new understanding on our hearts. Left to our own devices, we will fall for the culture's cheap imitations of love, which are based on physical attraction and emotional hunger.

Any attempt to love another without having first received love and experienced its true nature is ill advised. That's not to say we must be loved by others before we can love them. By no means! We should regularly act in loving ways toward people who are not loving toward us. But as individuals born with a sin nature into a fallen world, we must first receive real love before we can truly give it to anyone. Ideally, this begins as we recognize and receive love from the God who is love. Having our eyes opened to His grace and sacrificial love, we can learn to love Him in return and imitate His ways.

Indeed, we must put this love into practice in this world, for we cannot truly love God without learning to love others. For one thing, loving others is the primary vehicle God has put in place to help us understand His amazing love. As I experience the struggle, failure, and difficulty of loving broken and flawed people who don't always love me back, I grow a deeper appreciation of God's perfect love for me—a broken and flawed person who was once His enemy (Romans 5:8–10). This process begins in the place we call home.

Home is where husbands and wives attempt to love each other through both small and significant issues.

Home is where children are best raised in a culture of love that names fear for what it is and refuses to be ruled by it.

Home is where we lay down our lives in service to the friends we not only spend our time with, but who we also share the private sides of our lives with as well as invite to hold us accountable.

Home also extends to the workplace, where colleagues are more than just coworkers but form a work family.

Home includes our local church, our social groups, our community, and our nation—people with whom we spend our time and from whom we draw energy as we learn to love one another in response to God's love.

Listening and Loving

When we think of love, we often associate it with the heart. We don't talk about our brains skipping a beat when we meet the love of our life. We don't give kidney-shaped valentines in February or speak of suffering a broken stomach when we're grieving the loss of a loved one. Instead, poets and philosophers have written for millennia of love residing in the human heart.

I would like to suggest, however, that more than the heart, love ought to be associated with the ear. Why? Love listens. Consider this bit of wisdom from Dietrich Bonhoeffer's classic book *Life Together*:

> The first service one owes to others in the fellowship consists in listening to them.... It is God's love for us that He not only gives us His Word but also lends us His ear. So it is His work that we do for our brother when we learn to listen to him.[1]

Listening is a great act of love. It requires us to restrain our tongue, focus our attention, hear the other person's words, work to comprehend their meaning, and process what the person is trying to communicate. When we honestly and intently listen to others—not to debate them but to understand them—we are loving them.

Sadly, the home is sometimes the hardest place for a person to be heard. You're probably familiar with the saying that familiarity breeds contempt. As time goes by, it becomes easier to take a spouse for granted, thinking we already know what that person believes and what he or she will say. And so we stop listening for each other's unique perspective, and the marriage drifts into a deafening silence that is not conducive to intimacy.

The issues are somewhat different between parent and child, but the end results are similar. The culprit here is often our old adversary, busyness. Many parents allow themselves to get so busy that they fail to listen to their young children. Taking their parents' example, as the children age, they too get busy and stop listening to their parents.

The home should be a place where we learn to listen, but we must take the time and make the effort. Even when we have failed to listen and a breakdown in communication occurs, we can learn from the experience. We can stop and change course by recognizing the dangers of making assumptions and noticing the problems that arise when we fail to listen. As we learn to better listen to the ones we love, we will learn to better love those we encounter outside the home.

Building the Home of the Brave

As we have seen, the Home of the Afraid is ruled by fear. Every action is driven by it, and every attitude is dictated by it, even if subtly. The Home of the Brave, on the other hand, displaces fear with a different driver, and its name is Love. Being a "fearless family" does not mean we never experience fear; rather, it means we refuse to let fear determine our actions or attitudes. Instead, we choose the way of love. Consistently, imperfectly, but with great hope, we seek to discover and implement a way of doing things that is radically different from what comes naturally to us.

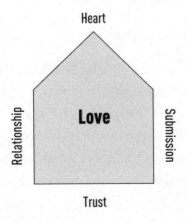

Whereas fear causes us to trust in safety, appearances, materialism, and power, love has different values. The walls in the Home of the Brave—connection to community and submission to one another—are far more healthy and reliable. Instead of seeking shelter under a roof of appearances, we pursue comfort by looking inside and focusing on the heart. But it all begins by building our lives on a different foundation.

The Foundation of Trust

While we discern safety and seek to avoid unnecessary risk, the Home of the Brave is not built on the false foundation of safety. Rather, we choose to anchor everything on a foundation of trust. We trust God while learning to trust one another. Trust expresses itself in a confident belief that God knows the best way, and while following Him may not always be easy, it will ultimately work for our good. We build trust in one another by knowing that although none of us will be perfect, we will make the choice each day to love one another.

The Roof of Heart

The Home of the Brave is covered by the roof of heart, or truth. Rather than putting our energies toward creating false outward appearances, we seek to know, understand, and live by the truth. This entails maintaining a dogged focus on building individual character and the character of our homes. We know that true transformation begins with choosing and teaching healthy heart attitudes instead of worrying about how others perceive us or what we are projecting to the world.

The Wall of Relationship

The first wall of the Home of the Brave is relationship. Instead of seeking comfort and protection from material things, we instead build and maintain constant connections with God, one another, our local church, and the neighbors in our community and around the world. Whereas fear always isolates us, love draws us together. We appreciate our shared needs. We seek to encourage one another, love one another, and forgive one another and learn to depend on one another as a way to ease our fears (Ephesians 4:32).

The Wall of Submission

The second wall of the Home of the Brave is submission. Rather than seeking control and power for ourselves, we find identity and opportunity in submitting to one another. We submit our lives to God and His command to think more highly of others than ourselves. We seek to serve others every day, knowing that in our acts of service, love will grow and cause fear to dissipate.

This is the way of love.

Think on These Things

1. Do you struggle more with loving or being loved? Why? What can you do this week to take a small step out of your comfort zone in this area?

2. How does listening communicate love to others? Would the members of your family say that they feel you really listen to them? What about your friends or colleagues? How about the strangers you meet?

3. Think of someone you have offended or injured in some way. Why is there nothing you can say or do that can ever fully repay that person or make up for your actions?

4. Think of someone among your family or friends who has difficulty trying new things or dealing with failure. What are some things you can do, starting right now, that can make this person more confident that you will love him or her no matter whether he or she succeeds or fails?

Chapter 7

Trust: The Foundation That Stands

You keep him in perfect peace whose mind is
stayed on you, because he trusts in you.

Isaiah 26:3

Do not be anxious about anything, but in everything by prayer and
supplication with thanksgiving let your requests be made known
to God. And the peace of God, which surpasses all understanding,
will guard your hearts and your minds in Christ Jesus.

Philippians 4:6–7

Most of us try to build our lives on a foundation of safety. Why? Because fear tells us we cannot truly be at peace until our safety and the safety of our loved ones are fully secured. So we run about battening down the hatches and making plans for any contingency. But reality has a way of rearing its head and, with a roar, reminding us that no matter how discerning, wise, and prudent we are, true safety will never be in our grasp.

Continually reaching for something we can never fully attain is a recipe for anxiety. The things we depend on to calm our fears only create more fear. Safety is not a strong foundation for a family home. But trust is.

The Home of the Brave is constructed on a foundation of trust. Knowing we can't fully secure safety for ourselves, we turn our attention instead to developing a deeper trust in God while also learning to trust one another.

Trusting God's Control

Flashback to several years ago: I am sitting on a beach and watching my six-year-old son play in the ocean. "I'll be fine, Dad," he tells me, but he doesn't have a clue what he's talking about. Silas knows nothing of the power of the ocean and what it's capable of. Sharks look cool and menacing on the Discovery Channel, but my son thinks he can just swim away from them. In the movies, the waves are made to be surfed; my son doesn't know they can easily dash him on the rocks or sweep him out to sea. Rip currents are as unknown to him as they are unseen to the rest of us.

The First Level of Awareness

As he played in the ocean that day, my son's defense readiness was at DEFCON 5, the lowest level of alert and awareness. This level of awareness boldly says, "I rule the ocean." Thinking he could jump the swells, ride the waves, or do whatever he wanted in the water on that calm, sunny day, my son rather foolishly believed he was in control of his surroundings.

This is the first level of awareness.

In much the same way, when things appear to be running smoothly, many of us arrive at the foolish conclusion that we control our lives. Because nothing terrible has happened to us during this relatively calm season, we think we're in charge and we know what we're doing. Not only is this naïve, but this silly notion often puts us in mind to judge others. After all, if we're controlling our lives, then others must be in control of theirs, right? So if something bad happens to them, it must be their fault. With this attitude, we don't see others' poverty, illness, and broken relationships in the context of systems, cultures, or harsh circumstances. Rather, we see these things as life choices. We foolishly believe that since we aren't poor or sick or divorced, other people shouldn't choose to be either.

> Safety is not a strong foundation
> for a family home. But trust is.

The Second Level of Awareness

It wouldn't have taken much to shake Silas from his throne and displace his six-year-old logic with a more realistic view of the ocean. A big enough wave, a strong enough current, or a sudden storm would immediately get his attention and raise his alert level. This heightened level of awareness says, "The ocean controls me." Anyone with a little experience in the water knows that a human has no control over the ocean. We might be able to play on its shores, ride its waves with a little practice, or explore its depths with the right equipment, but we cannot control the ocean. The ocean is dangerous and powerful and can do with us whatever it wants. Every sea captain knows this. Every person living on the beach understands this.

This is the second level of awareness.

It's easy in this world for life to suddenly feel out of our control. A scary diagnosis, an unexplained job loss, a broken relationship, the death of a parent, or the illness of a spouse or child can open our eyes to our own frailty and inability to control our circumstances. It can be a helpless, hopeless feeling. To fall from the heights of feeling totally in control and collide with the cold, hard truth of our absolute powerlessness is one of life's most frightening experiences. This terrifying realization is inevitable, but it is the beginning of maturity. Believing we control everything is foolish. Admitting we control very little is far wiser.

The Third Level of Awareness

Most people spend their lives either arrogantly believing they are in full control of their lives or, at the other extreme, dreadfully existing in the belief that their lives are completely beyond their control and subject to the whims of chance or fate. But a few of us realize the deepest of life's truths.

This third level of awareness says, "God is in control of the ocean."

While life, nature, and the world are not under our control, God is more powerful than all these things. Just because life doesn't always make sense to us does not mean there is no sense in living. God's sovereign control over His creation infuses our lives with meaning and purpose. For those of us who acknowledge His sovereignty and authority in our lives and submit to His will out of love and respect, God promises to bring good out of even our worst circumstances (Romans 8:28).

Living at level one of awareness as an adult is a choice born of arrogance or ignorance. It will ensure foolish action on our part and cause us to judge others unfairly. Those stubbornly living at level one have a deep trust of their own mastery, wisdom, and abilities—a trust that cannot be justified.

Living at level two of awareness ultimately is a choice born of deep apathy or despair. It will lead us to passivity and an overwhelming sense of the futility of life. Those living at level two trust no one.

Living at level three of awareness inspires hope and gives our lives meaning. It requires that we exercise faith in every circumstance of life, but it also enables us to endure no matter what comes our way. Those living at level three trust in God's sovereignty and goodness.

If you foolishly believe that you have control over every aspect of your life—wake up! You aren't that powerful. Nobody is.

If you sadly believe that life has no significance and that nothing you do really matters—look up! Your life has more purpose and potential than you think.

If you rightly believe that a loving God is in control of all things—speak up! The world needs to hear of your faith, to know that God is at work even in the midst of the most difficult circumstances.

The Home of the Brave is built on this third level of awareness, where it's understood that the by-product of knowing God is growing trust. This trust is buoyed by the hope that comes from recognizing that God is in control, that He has plans for our lives, and that He can and will use everything for His glory and our good.

Even in the most desperate of times, we can live in expectation that God is up to something good.

Trust Expressed in Obedience

Like love, trust is much more than a mere feeling. Like love, trust is best expressed in an action (or inaction, if required). The Home of the Brave is built on a foundation of radical trust in God. Knowing He is in control, we attempt to live each day in obedience to Him, whether or not we understand His plans for us. Even when we feel as if His commands are too demanding or we think His direction is an illogical approach to solving a specific problem, we nevertheless choose to obey Him because we trust in His unfailing love and infinite wisdom.

This means attempting to obey God as individuals while also learning what it means to obey Him collectively—as a family, as an organization, as a church, as a country. This applies in every area of life, but let's consider three specific areas in which we are called to obey: forgiveness, joyfulness, and generosity. Three of the most contrarian commands of God are for His people to forgive those who hurt us, to be joyful in the midst of our worst circumstances, and to be generous in the midst of a culture that is greedy.

Forgiveness

Building our homes on a foundation of trust means that we must regularly practice forgiveness. The ability and willingness to forgive are cornerstones of who we want to be. Let's face it, offenses in this life are guaranteed: we are certain to offend others, and we are certain to be offended. Having received God's forgiveness, we must offer forgiveness to others (Matthew 6:14–15; Colossians 3:13). But in order to forgive, we must do something that fear tells us to avoid—confront wrongs.

We can't truly forgive unless we first admit we were hurt, communicate our pain, and offer forgiveness to the one who has offended us. Whether or not the person accepts our forgiveness is up to him or her, but we must offer it. This doesn't mean we are required to continue a relationship with this individual or that we can't practice discernment when interacting with that person in the future, but it does mean we have to release the offender from the pain he or she has caused us. This is not easy. The greater the pain, the more difficult it is to forgive the person who caused it.

Of course, fear says we should hold a grudge. It tells us to hold on to our hurt as a way to have power over the other person, protect ourselves from future pain, and maybe even get payback somewhere down the road.

But God commands that we forgive, and so we do. We admit the hurt to ourselves, do the work to recognize its ramifications, have the difficult conversation in which we admit our pain to the person who caused it, and seek to reconcile the situation. In cases where we have caused pain to others, obedience means that we admit fault and seek their forgiveness even though we can't undo what we have done (Matthew 5:23–24).

Joyfulness

Trusting God and obeying Him means being joyful even through the difficult seasons and tougher moments of life. "Rejoice" is a common command throughout Scripture. In fact, Paul was rather insistent on this point of obedience (Philippians 4:4).

We are called to continually put joy back into our circumstances by remembering God's goodness, recognizing that His ways are higher than ours, and trusting that, in the end, all things will work out for our good. This means we are not to wallow in pity, worry about things we cannot control, or allow the sorrows of life to overtake the joy of our salvation. The Word is not telling us that we have to fake happiness at all times. Rejoicing in what God has done for us is not a call to stoicism or denial but is an invitation to live in a truth that is bigger than our current condition. This takes trust, and it requires obedience.

Generosity

As we have seen, fear drives us toward greed and materialism. Love, however, calls us to live generously. One practical step toward protecting ourselves from greed—and reminding ourselves that God is in control—is consistent and disciplined giving.

The Home of the Brave does not live off every dollar the family earns. Instead, we offer our tithes and more, trusting that God can accomplish more with 90 percent of our income than we can with 100 percent. We give as an act of obedience, trusting that the Lord's way is better both now and in the long run (Proverbs 3:9–10; 1 Timothy 6:18–19).

To the residents of the Home of the Afraid, this kind of generosity is foolish. We don't know what tomorrow holds, so fear says we must obtain as much as we can; fear says we can't trust others, so we must consume everything possible. But those who live in the Home of the Brave trust God and reject fear and so give freely and cheerfully.

These are just a few examples of how the fearless family expresses trust. Every day, each member submits both individually and collectively to a higher authority. We are not in charge of our own lives, for we have given the reins to God and therefore no longer determine for ourselves our next course of action.

God Is ...

How do we know we can trust God? Trusting God means knowing, understanding, and embracing the truth that:

- **God is always good.** Everything He does comes from a heart of love (Psalms 107:1; 145:9). He's not a grumpy old man trying to keep us off His lawn. He doesn't give arbitrary commands to keep us from having fun or to make our lives miserable. He wasn't trying to limit the lives of Adam and Eve by telling them what not to eat; He was telling them how to best live the life He gave them. So it is for us. Every command is an invitation to greater life. We can always know that God is working for our good (Psalm 84:11).
- **God is always powerful.** He is sovereignly in control. Nothing happens in our lives without His divine permission, if not by His divine direction (Ephesians 1:11). Even the most horrific of circumstances in our lives can be endured in the knowledge that God can and will use those situations for our good and His glory (Romans 8:28).

Rather than worrying or complaining, we need to be praying because we know that all things are in His hands and He is up to the task.

- **God is always right.** We never have to doubt this fact. Even if we can't understand what's happening in our lives, we can trust that the way of Jesus is the best way to live (Proverbs 3:5–6). To love our enemies may be difficult, but it's best (Matthew 5:44). To forgive when others offend us may not feel like the greatest move, but it is right (Colossians 3:13). Because God is all-knowing and always right, we should continually be studying what He says about how to live and applying His teachings to our lives (Hebrews 4:13; 2 Corinthians 5:9).

We can know and trust many things about God, but knowing that He is always good, always powerful, and always right are truths that will empower us through every situation.

Trusting One Another

Building our homes on a foundation of trust doesn't just mean we trust God. It also means we learn to trust and be trusted by one another. If it feels risky to trust God when He is all-powerful, then it must be crazy to trust others, because people are imperfect. Even with the best intentions, we will fail one another now and then. And when our intentions are bad, we can deeply injure one another. Yet trust is worth it.

All relationships are built on trust. Where trust isn't present, meaningful relationships aren't either. This demands that the Home of the Brave courageously chooses trust. Even though we will fail one another sometimes, we must learn to develop trust. And this requires that we value and diligently practice two important qualities—truth and commitment.

Trust is built on truth and commitment. Of course, it's tempting to think that human relationships would be much easier without them. If no one insisted on truth and commitment, our relationships would demand much less time, energy, and thought. They would create less discomfort, frustration, and friction. In fact, truth and commitment are *so* demanding that many people attempt to carry on meaningful relationships without either of them. The problem is, no relationship is meaningful without both.

Relationships depend on trust, and for trust to flourish, these two elements must be present. Without both, a relationship may appear meaningful on the surface but lack the depth of honesty and meaning. Truth and commitment are the difference between two people being acquaintances as opposed to actual friends. They're the difference between being roommates with the same last name as opposed to husband and wife, the difference between being parents and their child as opposed to legal guardians and their ward. Yet both truth and commitment complicate our lives enough that we often try to omit them from our relationships.

The Problem with Truth

The difficulty with truth is that it creates conflict. As long as I can lie without getting caught, I never have to experience friction in our relationship. I can pretend to agree with you, act as if everything's okay, and fool you into believing that I'm being real. While our interactions will be smooth, the relationship will be fake.

A real relationship demands honesty. Whether in friendship or marriage, we need to show our true hearts to each other in order to have a real connection. Without honesty, it's a pseudo-relationship. It might be easier to get along this way, but by hiding our thoughts, opinions, and beliefs, we are refusing to fully engage with the other person.

The other person deserves the truth. He or she has a right to assume you are investing your whole self. That doesn't mean you must be brutal or hurtful. Truth should only be shared within the context of love, but it does mean that you engage the totality of who you are. Instead of lying, evading, or deceiving, courageously confront reality, the truth, and facts. Only when two people interact with the truth can trust be present.

The Problem with Commitment

The trouble with commitment is that it demands we stay in a relationship when things aren't easy. It forces us to engage when we want to run, to confront when we want to hide, and to keep working at it when we want to give up. Commitment will cause you to have conversations you don't want to have. When others run from the issues, being committed to someone forces us to talk, listen, seek understanding, forgive, and reconcile.

The absence of commitment results in a string of broken relationships. We stay with people for as long as they make us feel good, but the moment there's a strain in the connection, we move on to another friendship, partnership, or marriage. But our friends, partners, and spouses deserve better. They should understand that they can't walk all over us, but they should also know that we won't run away at their first mistake. They should find comfort in knowing we will be full of grace whenever they need it.

Trust demands commitment. If I live in fear that you might abandon me because things are rough at the moment or because the truth hurts or because there is a better option somewhere else, I will neither invest my full heart in our relationship nor fully reveal myself to you. Instead, I will forever hold back part of myself (1) for fear that if you don't like what you see, you might leave, or (2) to protect myself so in case you do leave, that part of me won't have loved you anyway. So you see, without commitment, trust between us just isn't possible.

When Truth Weds Commitment

Trust is characterized by both truth and commitment. They feed off each other. Commitment woos truth out of hiding, and truth confirms that commitment is real. When both are present, couples, families, friends, and coworkers feel empowered to handle whatever comes their way. When either truth or commitment is missing, the relationship morphs into a false form.

Sadly, many people avoid both elements out of fear. Instead of trusting, they choose the appearance of safety. Having experienced heartbreak in the past, they write a false narrative that avoiding the truth and/or commitment will protect their heart from sorrow. But all it does is rob them of any chance of a real relationship.

However, when truth and commitment are wedded together, relationships flourish.

The marriage of a couple who embrace truth and commitment together will be fortified against outside threats. Every conflict will drive them closer to each other as they learn the value of both qualities.

When parents model truth and commitment for their children, their kids will learn (albeit with the occasional failure) to value truth and family both now and in the future. Also, the parent-child dynamic will be better equipped to evolve into a more mature relationship as the children reach adulthood.

As in a marriage, a friendship will be tested occasionally by misunderstanding, frustration, and friction. But if two people deal with the issues rather than deny their presence, they will learn to trust each other more.

In business, nothing hurts productivity and success in a company like failing to face facts. When an organization trains its employees to live in deception—for example, rewarding a manager who exaggerates his department's productivity or blames others to cover up his mistakes—the company's bottom line is inevitably damaged. But when employees are empowered to confront the truth and work through it, the possibilities are endless.

On the face of it, it's easier to conceal our hearts and difficult truths and engage in surface-level relationships. By doing so, we hope that life won't hurt as much. However, nothing contributes to a person's emotional well-being, life satisfaction, and overall happiness like meaningful relationships. To experience a life-changing connection, we must deal with the truth. To handle the truth, we need commitment, because without it we'll be tempted to run as soon as things get uncomfortable. When truth and commitment are present, trust is possible.

Using Discernment

People aren't perfect and sometimes they will disappoint us. So for us to trust anyone, we will have to be able to forgive and have the courage to trust those who have failed us. Every time my children lie to me, I explain to them that our relationship is built on trust. When they lie, it causes me to question and doubt them, and this gets in the way of our relationship.

Of course, knowing how much it hurts me when they lie, I'm careful not to lie to them. This is true even when it's tempting to be deceitful for their own good. Parenting an introvert, I often have to negotiate to get him to go into new settings. "If you go, I'll pick you up in an hour," I say. Knowing once he gets there he will have fun, I'm tempted to pick him up later than what I promised. But being true to my word is more important. I never want to give them a reason to doubt me, so I stick to my word. Long-term trustworthiness is more valuable than any temporary desire. When one of us fails to tell the truth, we must confront it, forgive it, and try to do better the next time.

However, some failures with the truth cannot be repaired immediately. Trust between two people isn't blindly given; it's earned. When trust is violated, it can take time to repair. And in some cases, it simply can't be repaired. Where addiction is present, so is deceit. Where adultery happens, many couples find the ability to trust each other again, but some don't. Some choose not to, and that is their right. Too often there comes a point where it's nearly impossible to restore trust between two people.

> Trust between two people isn't
> blindly given; it's earned.

All of this requires discernment. What's the difference between an easily forgiven failure to tell the truth versus a more serious violation where trust should not be restored swiftly? Both lies are wrong, but they likely have different outcomes. We should be quick to trust and extend grace, but we shouldn't be hasty in choosing where we put our trust. Some people have not earned our trust, while others may have destroyed our trust completely.

Being Trustworthy

We know how difficult it can be to trust others after we've been hurt, used, and manipulated. It's natural for us to want to protect our hearts by not fully trusting, yet the fearless family recognizes the value of trust and its importance for healthy relationships, and so we seek to trust. However, we also must work toward being trustworthy ourselves.

We build trustworthiness by developing and maintaining several important habits:

- **We don't lie.** Nothing sows distrust like falsehoods. Even when we tell a "little white lie," it gives the appearance that we have something major to hide. Yet a majority of the lies we tell are not about trying to cover up a major sin. Most of the time we lie out of laziness, insecurity, or pride. Sometimes telling the truth takes effort whereas a little lie seems simpler. Sometimes we fear that the other person might judge us if he or she knew the truth. Sometimes we lie because we think the other person can't understand or handle the truth. No matter the reason, every lie comes at a price. The truth is always better.

- **We don't tell half-truths.** Sometimes we try to masquerade the whole truth by telling a half-truth. Many people are skilled at "technically" not lying. While they can claim, "I never said ...," the truth is, they misled the other person by telling only a partial truth. These foolish games are just as wrong and costly as lying.

- **We recognize the insecurities of others.** We all have struggles, doubts, and hurtful past experiences. In order to be trustworthy, not only do we have to tell the truth, but we also have to recognize the hurts of others. When someone has been lied to in the past or greatly hurt by the deceit of another, he or she may be highly vulnerable. In such a case, being trustworthy not only requires that we tell the truth, but also that we might need to go to extra lengths to comfort this person's doubts. Without complaint or grumbling, we may need to offer him or her more assurances, communicate more clearly about our whereabouts, etc.

Take a Risk and Give the Gift of Trust

Trust is something we all desire to have but few desire to give. It's a precious commodity and one that can be costly when we give it to others. After all, it's hard to feel abandoned unless we trusted others to be there for us. It's hard to feel betrayed unless we trusted others to be on our side. It's hard to be disappointed unless we trusted others to do what they said they would.

Previous experiences with violations of trust can hinder our personal relationships, but more importantly, they can impede our faith. Faith without trust is no faith at all. The very nature of belief is that we place our trust in God. We trust Him to forgive our sins, deliver us from evil, and lead us into goodness. We trust Him with everything we have and are.

Our trust is the greatest gift we have to give, both to God and to others. The Home of the Brave simply cannot stand without our trust. So choose to let go of your fears, take a risk, and give the gift of trust.

Think on These Things

1. Consider the title of the old hymn "Trust and Obey." Can we do one without the other? Is it possible to trust God and not obey Him or to obey God and not trust Him? Why, or why not?

2. Trusting God requires us to understand and believe that God is always good, always powerful, and always right. Which of these have you struggled most to believe? Why?

3. Would your family and friends say that you are trustworthy? Do you have a tendency to stretch or withhold the truth from your loved ones? Think of a recent instance in which you lied to someone, even if it was a little lie. How did you rationalize the lie to yourself?

4. How might your home be different if your family began showing an unwavering trust in God and a growing trust in one another?

Chapter 8

Heart: Above All Else

I know, my God, that you test the heart and are pleased with integrity.

1 Chronicles 29:17 NIV

Above all else, guard your heart, for everything you do flows from it.

Proverbs 4:23 NIV

Cosmetic surgery versus cardiology. That's the difference between the Home of the Afraid and the Home of the Brave. Whereas plastic surgery is an important branch of medicine involving the restoration and reconstruction of injured, lost, or diseased tissue, cosmetic surgery is all about enhancing appearances. Cardiology, on the other hand, is all about healing the heart.

Without a heartbeat, nothing else matters. That's one reason why cardiology and pulmonology are far ahead of neurology in terms of our medical understanding. The brain is essential, but without a heart pushing blood to the brain and oxygen delivering air to the brain, the intricate functions of the brain don't matter as much. To the human body, the heart matters more than the face. The same is true in our homes.

The Home of the Brave dwells under the shelter of heart. There our fixation is not so much on the face we show to the world but rather on the content of our heart and what it says about who we are.

The Home of the Afraid seeks refuge under the leaky roof of appearances. We think that pretending to be something we're not will somehow lessen our fears, but it doesn't. Instead, our anxieties increase as we desperately try to control what others think of us, always aware that our true selves could be exposed at any moment. Meanwhile, we battle the incessant guilt from knowing that we are not who we think we should be. Staying on the treadmill of keeping up appearances is exhausting.

The Home of the Brave requires that we make a different choice. There we feel the fear and understand the temptation to mislead others as to who we are, but we choose instead the way of love. Trusting God and one another, we feel an obligation toward the truth. We know that as we seek truth and live by the truth, we can experience freedom. We still care about our reputation, of course; we always desire a good name. But we don't base our lives and actions on the opinions of others. We spend our time instead on strengthening our character and encouraging those with whom we find friendship. We spend so much time and energy on improving the heart that we don't have time to think about the face.

Defining the Heart

We use the word *heart* metaphorically to mean many different things. For example, we often use it to speak of love. Saying "She stole my heart" communicates romantic affections. *Heart* is commonly used to define one's endurance or ability to persevere. An athlete who always hustles is said to play with real heart. When people are suffering and tempted to give up, we encourage them not to lose heart. We also use the word to refer to a person's character or integrity. Saying "She has a good heart" means that she chooses to love no matter the circumstances, or that she stands by her convictions when others are going along with the crowd. Getting to "the heart of the matter" means focusing on the most important, basic, or essential elements of an issue or problem and can describe an admirable decision-making process.

In the Home of the Brave, the word *heart* implies all of these things. Valuing heart over appearances means we care about our character, our motives, our endurance, our relationships, and the reality of who we are far more than the perception others might have of us.

Integrity: It's Time to Bring It Back

In a society that honors power, wealth, and fame, one quality is often overlooked that should be valued and desired over any of these others: integrity. If I had to pick one attribute for my children to achieve in life, ranking higher than health or wealth would be the presence of character in their lives.

> If I had to pick one attribute for my children to achieve in life, ranking higher than health or wealth would be the presence of character in their lives.

While an absence of integrity has always been a problem in this world, humanity may have never experienced a time in which the concept of character is so ignored or downplayed. We have grown to expect corruption, deceit, and dishonesty from politicians, the media, companies, coworkers, institutions, churches, spouses, and friends. Pessimism and cynicism so define this culture, many of us are convinced that having integrity isn't even possible anymore.

But it is. I regularly interact with people of fantastic character. That doesn't mean they're perfect, nor does it mean I'm never surprised or disappointed by poor choices they've made. What it does mean is that most of the time, these people make the hard but right decisions, perform noble deeds, and demonstrate an internal strength that many no longer believe exists.

One problem with modern society's skeptical view of character is that because people no longer believe it's possible to walk with integrity, they don't teach it to their children. Many parents, schools, and even churches don't bother with character training, nor do the adults model for kids how to earn a good reputation. In our cynicism, we create a self-fulfilling prophecy. We assume good character is a thing of the past, and so we fail to pursue integrity ourselves or pass it on to our children.

Thankfully, our pessimism is unfounded. Good character still exists, and it can be taught and learned. And we aren't being hypocrites in demanding integrity from our leaders and others when we're not always perfect ourselves. As a matter of fact, integrity is not about perfection. In some ways, it has more to do with how to deal with our *im*perfections.

Five Signs of Integrity

Integrity, or character, can be evident in a person's life in a number of ways. Here are five simple characteristics to look for—and work on—in the Home of the Brave.

1. Say what you mean. I don't know anyone who values integrity but believes that lying is acceptable. However, a lot of people who say they want to have good character regularly tell lies. Often, this involves saying yes when they mean no. Or they remain quiet, giving the appearance of consent when they actually disagree. They don't say no with their mouths, but they do so with their actions by failing to do what they have agreed to do. Having integrity means being trustworthy. If you mean no, say no (Matthew 5:37). Remember, it's fear that drives us to lie. We will frequently mislead people if fear prevents us from telling the whole truth.

2. Do what you say. Having integrity means being whole or complete. When something has integrity, it is undivided. Most often a lack of integrity is revealed when our words don't match our actions, as when we say one thing but do something else. But when a person consistently does what he says he will do, he demonstrates to everyone around him that he is whole and without divide.

3. Respect other people's time. An often overlooked aspect of integrity involves how we interact with others. Whenever we fail to respect another person, we show an absence of character. Respecting another person's time ties into doing what I say. If we have arranged to meet at a particular time or for a specific length of time, I must honor that.

4. Respect other people's decisions. Respecting a person's decision does not mean I agree with what she has decided, but it does mean I respect her right to make the decision. Without exercising control, manipulation, or codependency, people of integrity will understand which choices are theirs to make and which decisions are in the hands of others.

5. Admit your mistakes. Integrity has less to do with perfection and far more to do with how we handle imperfection—both ours and that of others. Nobody is perfect. Therefore, we shouldn't be shocked by personal failures. When they occur, a person of principle is quick to recognize them, admit them, and correct them. Integrity is often displayed through a sincere apology, genuine remorse, and a concerted effort to right the wrong. People who lack integrity downplay their faults, deny their failures, and dismiss the frustrations of others.

Being a person of strong character requires more than just these five characteristics, but they are a good start. Bad character can be hidden for a time; it's not all that difficult to deceive ourselves and others. But make no mistake: an absence of integrity will eventually reveal itself. When it does, the fallout can be devastating. However, few things are as stabilizing—to a family, community, organization, or country—as a person of strong character.

Imagine that I could give you a choice of whom your child could marry. One person is rich, famous, and outwardly very successful. The other is poor, unknown, and has little influence beyond a small circle of friends. But the first person has no integrity, while the second person is someone of great character. Whom would you wish your child to marry? Without question, I would choose the person of character. As we desire integrity in our children's lives, so we should seek it for ourselves. Character matters.

Family Character

When we think of integrity or character, we tend to think in terms of the individual, and rightly so. Character begins with the individual. However, families, social groups, and organizations (including churches) also have what might be called "corporate character." There is an assumed way in which decisions are made, people are treated, and the group functions. This is corporate character. For a group to have excellent character, it must be composed of individuals with excellent character. However, just because good people make up the group doesn't guarantee the group will have integrity. Reasonable people can overlook or turn a blind eye to collective character, and without intention, they can create a family unit, group, or organization that is unethical.

Leaders and residents in the Home of the Brave consider both individual integrity and corporate integrity. We regularly take stock of our own hearts and the heart of the group as a whole. When I sit with ministry and organizational leaders and discuss where we should spend our time and energy, we debate as to the types of issues and tasks that require a leader's personal attention and the kinds that should be passed on to others. I use the acronym CARE to remind leaders of those things that are ultimately their responsibility. A leader cannot delegate being accountable for the Character of the organization, calming the Anxieties of its employees and volunteers, deciding the Responsibilities of who does what, and driving the Energy of the organization. Most issues and tasks can be delegated, but these things can't.

While leaders can't control everything that happens within their family, group, or organization, they are responsible for how they respond to problems. Leaders who tolerate a lack of integrity within a group or company are threatening the integrity of their organization. Parents who condone poor behavior from family members are endangering the home.

Installing a roof of heart on the Home of the Brave begins with the development of strong character within the family. Character training is a process that never ends and must forever be at the forefront of our thinking. This makes it important for parents to determine how the family will operate. We need to define for ourselves and our children what we value and how we will live out those values. A friend of mine told me he created two simple rules for his home as his kids were growing up: don't lie and don't be lazy. He found that nearly every facet of life was covered by "the Two Ls." While these are good rules, what's more important is that they were clearly defined and communicated to all involved. If you want to live under the roof of heart, you must define what heart means to your family and then hold each person accountable for those things.

> A friend of mine told me he created two simple rules for his home as his kids were growing up: don't lie and don't be lazy.

Guarding and Keeping the Heart

Much of the book of Proverbs is written from the perspective of a father explaining life to his son. Chapter 4 is the first in a series of chapters in which he warns his son about the many significant moral dangers in the world. In one verse in particular, the father describes what should be the young man's ultimate focus: "Above all else, guard your heart" (Proverbs 4:23 NIV).

Many things matter in our approach to daily life. How we spend money, what we do with our time, how we prepare for the future, and so on. Yet above all other concerns, the fearless family recognizes the importance of guarding our hearts. An impure heart will taint everything. A dead or hardened heart will prevent any meaningful growth or action. For this reason, we must make heart health our highest priority.

Some translations of Proverbs 4:23 use the word *guard*, while others opt for *keep* to convey the writer's meaning. I like them both. The two words have similar meanings but with nuanced differences. We need to both guard *and* keep our hearts.

The word *guard* reminds us that our hearts are under attack daily. C. S. Lewis said we live in "enemy-occupied territory."[1] We have a very real, very wily opponent. And while we don't have to live in fear of that opponent, we should respect his ability. As a pastor, I see on an everyday basis the destruction that takes place when a heart is left unguarded and exposed to the whims of human passion or desire. Unaware of the danger, those who fail to guard their hearts walk a dangerous path.

We must be determined to protect our affections and desires. We have to set boundaries for ourselves so we can keep a clear head and make wise decisions. Remember, not everyone is rooting for you to succeed. The world has no interest in helping you to love your spouse more. Society certainly won't raise your children to keep a pure heart.

Our homes and families are under attack, and we must protect them. This requires guarding our hearts, for when our hearts fail, we fail.

We also need to "keep" our hearts, taking intentional steps to stay encouraged and motivated. We cannot allow world-weariness to cause our focus to drift, leaving our hearts vulnerable to attack.

As a pastor, I've watched many people die, but I'll never forget the first. I was in college and doing a chaplaincy internship. As I walked into the hospital on my first day, the chaplain I was to shadow said, "Follow me." We wound our way through the hospital as he introduced himself. He was talking fast, and I was hustling to keep up with both his words and his steps. As we rounded a corner, he came to a sudden stop and said, "Take a deep breath." Before I could even get air in my lungs, he pushed through a set of double doors and we entered an operating room.

Orderlies were washing blood off the floor, while nurses were cleaning up a body. Suddenly, we heard screams coming from the other room. The surgeon had just told the family that their patriarch had died during a routine medical procedure. Death isn't unusual in a hospital, but this one was quite unexpected. The surgical team was heartbroken that an everyday procedure had gone terribly wrong. The patient's family was in shock; they hadn't even expected their father to remain overnight in the hospital.

The chaplain I was with moved from person to person, trying to provide as much comfort as possible. After some time, everyone began to go his own way, then we left. The chaplain was obviously exhausted. As we walked back to his office, he said, "Hey, I want to show you something." Soon we stood outside another set of double doors. "No need for a deep breath here," he said. He pushed through, and I found myself in front of a large window with several newborn babies on the other side. This was the nursery. The chaplain said, "Anytime you face a difficult case in the hospital, it's always a good idea to run by here to remind yourself that while there is a lot of sorrow in the world, there is also a lot of good. While there is death, there is also life." In that moment, the chaplain was teaching me how to keep my heart.

Life is hard. Marriage is difficult. Parenting is demanding. Leadership can suck the life out of you. We all need encouragement, and on occasion, we need to be reminded of the good in the world. Sorrow is so powerful that when we experience it, we can feel as though it's the only thing in the world. If we don't keep heart, then time, pain, grief, sorrow, loss, disappointment, and failure will erode our ability to fend off the attacks of the enemy. But if we do, then we will become overwhelmed by life.

Building the Home of the Brave requires that we find ways to encourage one another, to keep the big picture before us, and to instill hope in ourselves and others. As a father, I must remind myself that my most significant task is to inspire godly hope in the lives of my children. I have to tell them of the goodness of God, His constant presence in our lives, and His ongoing work on our behalf. To instill godly hope, I must have godly hope. To have it, I must cultivate it by reminding myself of the truth, interacting with God daily, being encouraged by others, and forming habits and disciplines that will nourish my soul.

Above all else, I must guard and keep my heart and theirs.

Heart and Mission

In the movies, Shrek and Donkey were transformed by their journey together and a quest to rescue first a princess and then a kingdom. Rocky Balboa fell short in his shot at the title but, through perseverance and heart, nonetheless grew into a champion. A great team overcomes adversity to earn a chance at winning a championship.

Mission and heart go hand in hand. In art and in life, heroes learn what they are made of in the course of a difficult journey, and their quest helps to make them more than what they were. Show me someone with a great heart, and I'll show you someone who recognizes a sense of purpose in his or her life. Character is created for mission, and mission creates heart. The relationship is reciprocal.

Heart Is Created *for* the Mission

There is always a higher purpose beyond ourselves. We focus on ourselves so we may then forget about ourselves in the pursuit of a greater good. If a public speaker doesn't recognize her nervousness before an engagement and find a way to channel that nervous energy in a good way, she will find it difficult to focus on her audience or the speech she is giving. She must examine herself *before* the mission so she doesn't spend her whole time during the mission trying to compensate for her weaknesses. So it is with any leader. We work on our character as a part of preparing for a greater mission. This is also the reason we focus on the character of the family members and individuals we lead.

A coach is quick to point out any laziness he sees in a player during the preparation phase. The laziness is a character flaw; it's a failure to put in the heart and work necessary to accomplish a task. A good coach will show the player how laziness will hinder both the player and the team in the pursuit of victory. Lazy practice habits lead to lazy in-game habits, which can lead to a loss for the team. Character development is always linked to the pursuit of a mission.

As parents and Christians, we need good character because of the great tasks before us. Unless you communicate the significance of the mission, your children may never come to realize the importance of integrity, honesty, courage, and other valuable qualities. When a child demonstrates apathy toward character development, it reveals the parents' failure to convey the importance of the mission accurately.

Heart Is Created *by* the Mission

The pursuit of something important motivates willingness to change and grow. If people believe passionately in the goal, they are willing to confront anything that might hinder their mission. But bad character frustrates every purpose. When a teammate can't be trusted or a parent lacks integrity or siblings look out for themselves over others, the group's performance suffers. Good character creates good teams; bad character leads to dysfunctional teams.

Mission not only motivates us to change and grow; it also reveals what needs to change. Worthy pursuits exhaust us. They demand everything we have, wringing every ounce of energy from us. In the process, weaknesses are revealed. It's easy for team members to deceive themselves or others in times of ease. We can appear stronger than we really are. We may even think we have it all together. But the testing that comes from fighting to complete a critical mission strips away our delusions. Weak spots will appear, character flaws will emerge, and we will quickly realize our need to grow and improve. Only when we are pursuing a worthwhile mission will we truly expend ourselves to such an extent that our weaknesses will be fully revealed.

Hasn't the US Army understood this concept for years? Isn't this the idea behind basic training? Drill sergeants work to break down enlisted men and women in order to build them back into the best they can be. They pressure the mind and stress the body to identify which areas need improvement. Once weaknesses have revealed themselves, they can be confronted and addressed.

So many individuals, teams, and organizations fail to achieve their goals because they downplay the importance of character. In so doing, they set themselves up for defeat. You might be able to ignore character to gain a few short-term wins, but eventually, bad character will reveal itself and undermine both the individual and the team.

What does this look like in terms of a family? Are we supposed to pressure our kids, berate and belittle them, demand perfection, and push them to their breaking points? Of course not! But we do need to show them what they're capable of and teach them to expect more of themselves than they thought possible. We need to encourage them to keep trying when they fail and not to give up. We need to show them that they can achieve more by working together and encouraging one another than they could ever accomplish on their own (Ecclesiastes 4:9). And we need to teach them to understand and accept the importance of their mission as Christians and future parents and leaders. Perhaps above all, we need to teach our children that good character is an accomplishment and a gift that are to be used for the well-being of others.

The Heart and Trust Connection

There is a close relationship between the ceiling and floor in both the Home of the Afraid and the Home of the Brave. Without learning how to trust others and be trustworthy, it is far too risky to show people who we actually are. When safety is the foundation on which we build everything, appearances will quickly become the roof of our home. But when safety is replaced with trust, appearances give way to truth. Then we can build a foundation of trust and create a climate where we can courageously and honestly reveal our true hearts to one another.

I pastor a good number of recovering addicts. One of the most striking characteristics of people who have been walking the road of recovery for many years is how seriously they take the concept of truth-telling. Having lived in the grip of addiction, they know the dangers of deceit. Addicts are masterful liars, but recovery shows them the importance of telling the truth. Some of the most humbly honest people I know are recovering addicts.

"We tell the truth" is a foundational house rule that should be implemented by any parent who wants to create a loving and courageous home. Nothing reveals a healthy heart like consistently telling the truth. Keep in mind, however, that it takes time to cultivate a commitment to honesty. If your young child already has a habit of continually lying, be patient and don't feel guilty. A young person's ability to consistently tell the truth will grow as a result of being raised in a home where family members are taught to trust one another.

Saving Face or Changing Hearts?

Saving face versus changing hearts. That's the difference between the Home of the Afraid and the Home of the Brave. Fear worries about perception; love is concerned with reality.

What gives the fearless family perspective to focus on growing healthy hearts is their great trust in God. They understand that God is at work among them to change each individual as well as the whole. They believe that every circumstance and situation is an opportunity for them to learn more about themselves and more about God and to grow in character as they grow closer to one another. They can even embrace sorrow or disappointment because they trust that God will use it for their good. This adds a sense of excitement and expectation to even the most mundane of situations. For in the classroom of God, the Instructor never takes a moment off.

Does God care about our public faces? Of course. We don't have to live in total denial of what others think of us. But in the Home of the Brave, our faces are mere by-products of our hearts. If we don't like what others see, we don't spend too much time attempting to improve the visuals. Instead, we ask God to change our hearts and, in so doing, change what others see in us.

Think on These Things

1. Review the five signs of integrity. Which of these is an area where your family could show improvement? What can you do or emphasize this week to help your family take steps in the right direction?

2. Have you made character training a priority at home? Why, or why not? What character-related goals do you have for your children?

3. What kinds of circumstances cause you to become stressed or discouraged? What are some things you can do in order to make sure you don't lose heart in these circumstances?

4. What boundaries have you put in place to guard your heart and protect the hearts of your family?

Chapter 9

Relationship: Choosing People Over Things

*For the whole law is fulfilled in one word: "You
shall love your neighbor as yourself."*

Galatians 5:14

Let us not love with words or speech but with actions and in truth.

1 John 3:18 NIV

As an actor, Tom Hanks is considered something of an Everyman. Like Jimmy Stewart before him, Hanks is likable and wonderfully talented, but he doesn't possess a single defining characteristic that distinguishes him from all other screen performers. He's not a classic heartthrob, enticing women to flock to movie theaters. He's not athletically inclined in a way that makes men want to be him. He's funny, but he's not a stand-up comedian. (Does anybody remember *Punchline?*) He's smart, but he doesn't come across as having a towering intellect, which would make him inaccessible to most of us.

The gift of Tom Hanks is that he can play almost any character and have every person in the audience identify with him, see ourselves in him, or think, *I could be friends with that guy*.[1] He's an Everyman, and the movies he appears in tend to embrace messages that speak to the heart of humanity. Perhaps the most common theme running through his films is the importance of human connection.

The first Tom Hanks movie I ever saw was *Big* in which he played a child locked in a man's body. In the film, Hanks finds work at a toy company, where he interacts with a group of executives who are obsessed with turning profits, achieving success, and leapfrogging one another on the corporate ladder. But some of them are changed when Hanks reminds them of the importance of fun and real human connection.

Forrest Gump isn't a child, but he is a simple man with a knack for breaking down cultural barriers and creating friendship wherever he goes.

Saving Private Ryan and *Apollo 13* remind us of what we can accomplish when we accept an overwhelming challenge and tackle it with heart, determination, and sacrificial love for one another.

Toy Story, Sleepless in Seattle, The Green Mile, You've Got Mail, A Beautiful Day in the Neighborhood—all of these films remind us of humanity's deep-seated need for relationship and the individual's responsibility for reaching out and making it happen.

So many Tom Hanks movies are about the importance of human connection, but the movie that might illustrate it best is *Cast Away*. In this film, Hanks plays a time-obsessed systems engineer for FedEx who is the lone survivor of a plane crash somewhere in the Pacific Ocean. After washing ashore on a deserted island, along with a number of undelivered FedEx packages, Hanks struggles for four years to survive without any human interaction whatsoever. One of the packages contains a Wilson-brand volleyball. Lonely and desperate for companionship, Hanks begins to talk to the ball, which he addresses as Wilson.

When left without human connection, we will either find a way to create it or simply go mad. It's why some countries consider solitary confinement to be immoral. It's why when kids have behavioral issues, the first question parents should consider is the state of the child's relationships. It's why addiction is now seen more as a failure of the community than a lack of self-control.

People were created to love and be loved, so it's not surprising that we tend to flourish in a climate of love and support but languish when love is absent. And yet we often avoid personal attachments out of fear. Fear reminds us we are vulnerable and calls into question the motives of others. It causes us to focus our attention on what could go wrong should we dare to demonstrate love or—*gasp!*—open our hearts to others.

We've all experienced the heartbreak of love gone wrong. And many of us still deal with insecurities and injuries resulting from past relationships in which we were not loved as we should have been. Some of these old wounds have been with us since childhood. Even the best of parents don't love their children perfectly, and their best intentions can lead to unintended outcomes. Even healthy families experience conflict and the occasional breakdown in communication.

Then there are those of us who were raised in unhealthy homes or landed in toxic relationships where we were hurt by people with bad intentions. The amount of damage that can be done in the name of love is staggering. It's no wonder so many of us are terrified to seek out and experience real relationship.

The Mirage of Materialism

Needing love but fearing rejection or worse, we try a different way. Many of us believe we can find the love, support, and comfort we need in something other than a reciprocal relationship with real people. So we chase the mirage of materialism at the expense of human connection.

> We chase the mirage of materialism at the expense of human connection.

Whereas love calls us to use things and love people, fear drives us to use people and love things. It makes a kind of sense. A beautiful new car won't cause us heartbreak, but breaking up with a college sweetheart can hurt for years to come. A nice vacation won't scar our memories, but one unkind word from our grandmother can stay with us forever. A big-screen TV won't wound us emotionally, but betrayal by a best friend can be devastating.

We know all too well that we can't make it through life on our own. We understand that we need love and support. Yet instead of risking connection with others, we turn to things to find comfort, peace, and satisfaction. We believe that if we can find the right stuff, more stuff, better stuff, it can bring us the peace we need.

My son is strongly motivated by rewards, so my wife and I regularly discuss the minimum reward necessary to get him to do the desired action. It's incredible how quickly he can accomplish something when it's tied to the proper carrot. And yet, what drives him often comes up empty. He might do his chores or homework several days in a row without complaint to earn a small toy. But one day after receiving that toy, it's cast aside. It means nothing to him. He put great hope into what the toy might give him, but in the end, it brings him very little. Every time I see this played out in his childhood, I think about the different ways I do the same thing but with much more expensive toys.

Materialism is a mirage. We think we see something shimmering in the distance, but in reality it's nothing. We thirst for connection and meaning from our possessions and long for the items we don't already own, but those things can never provide us what we are looking for. This is because we are meant to connect with real, live humans. That's not to say material things are pointless; they do play roles in our lives. However, when we expect from material things what only other people can provide, we are setting ourselves up for great disappointment.

Love is a reflection of God, and it can ultimately be given only by God and those created in His image. We can love God, and we can love each other. Everything else is a mirage.

Where God Has Placed Us

God lives, and has always lived, in harmonious relationship. As three persons existing as one God, relationship is part of His very nature. So when He created mankind in His own image, He made us to live in relationship too. When God said, "It is not good for the man to be alone" (Genesis 2:18 NIV), it was a statement not just of one man's need for a wife but also humanity's need for one another. In fact, we were meant to enjoy with Him and among ourselves the kind of fellowship and unity that the Father, Son, and Holy Spirit have always known.

While we need and are meant to develop other relationships, the place we are designed to experience our first connections is inside a home. It's no accident that most of us were born into a family. While some children are born into isolation, everyone recognizes that this is wrong. It is among the greatest of tragedies when a newborn baby is abandoned. Not only were we meant to be raised in a family, but we were meant to be loved by others for months before we even enter the world.

Ideally, each of us is born into a loving and supportive family. As we grow, we learn from family, friends, and neighbors what it means to love and be loved. Then, when the time is right, we launch out on our own to begin our own families, where this process is then repeated. Of course, no one's situation is ideal. Everyone experiences heartaches and setbacks. Yet the basic design does not change—we still need connection and a sense of belonging.

If we're not experiencing that connection at home, then we need to set about trying to heal the home. We should seek help and make the effort to turn our homes into places of genuine meaning. We do that by first understanding how the Home of the Brave is properly constructed.

Connecting Trust and Heart

Thus far we have established a foundation of trust, and we have settled on the finest-grade roof of heart. Now we need two strong walls. The first wall, the wall of relationship, is a perfect fit and firmly joins the foundation of trust to the roof of heart.

The foundation of trust isn't just about trusting God; it's also about learning to trust others. Without trust, real connection with others is not possible. While trust is indeed earned, we must also be liberal in giving our trust to others even when it doesn't come naturally to us. Trusting others empowers us to make connections, and until we trust, we can't fully connect.

The wall of relationship also attaches to the roof of heart. But to make the connection between roof and wall strong, each person must bring his or her whole heart to the relationship. As long as we put our faith in appearances and work hard to project a fake persona, our relationships will be limited in terms of growth.

Far too many people are in a relationship with only part of a person or someone they don't even know. So many women are married to a man who has never fully put his heart into the relationship. They said "I do" to one person but find they are married to someone else. The man tries to maintain the aura of strength, competency, and completeness he brought into the marriage, but it's an act meant to ward off fear. The woman thinks she's married to the whole man, but she only ever experiences part of the man, the facade.

This is true of many relationships. We think we are connected to one person, but we are actually connected to someone else. This stunts relationship growth and eventually kills the connection, and often it happens without our knowledge. We don't know that the other person isn't offering us his or her full self.

And we're just as guilty. Worried about appearances, we let the other person see only a part of ourselves—the part we think is put together, attractive, or somehow admirable. And then we wonder why we're never entirely sure if the other person loves us or accepts us!

It's only when we begin to take risks and lay our full hearts on the table that we can ever hope to make a genuine connection with our loved ones. Letting our guard down and making ourselves vulnerable will enable us to engage fully in the relationship. Because we are no longer focused on projecting an attractive persona, we can focus instead on the other person. This allows us to love better and receive love in return.

Secure relationships strengthen trust and heart in both parties. The latter empowers the former, while the former further establishes the latter.

What Do We Value?

So how do we build this wall to be as strong as possible? While many of us are tempted to deny the importance of personal connection for safety's sake, love offers a different perspective.

Consider this working mom. She's overwhelmed with everything she wants and needs to get done. Meals have to be prepared. Laundry must be done. Homework has to be checked. A quick check of a child's backpack reveals mandatory participation in the science fair, which happens to be tomorrow. She also has a business to run. Clients are demanding, and project deadlines are fast approaching. It's also tax season, with all the paperwork that entails. Because of the myriad demands on her time and energy, it's easy for the mom to convince herself that she has no time for investing in relationships. And so her life becomes solely about production. Even the interactions she has with those closest to her are just about logistics: she asks her husband to pick up the kids from practice, she debates with the kids about chores that need to be done, she gives hurried instructions to her employees, and she texts with a friend about how she can contribute to a homeroom party or Sunday school get-together. But at no point does she actively engage in a relationship with someone.

But love will drive her a different way. It will cause her to recognize the value of relationships and choose to invest in them, even with all the other demands swirling around her. She will engage her husband in in-depth conversation that's about more than just who is picking up their kids or what's for dinner. She will take time to talk with her kids about something more than just their homework or extracurricular requirements. She will turn what might feel like a wasteful decision to have lunch with friends into an opportunity to open her heart to others and listen to God. Although she has no more hours in the day than before, love will motivate her to prioritize relationships over other responsibilities, even as fear tells her that meaningful connections are a luxury she doesn't have time for. She will choose to build a strong wall of relationship even if it means that other tasks go undone.

The choice boils down to value. Love calls us to value some things that others devalue and to devalue some things that others covet. Compare a diamond to an ordinary rock. Since the fourth century BC, when they were first mined in India, diamonds have been symbols of power and status. Because of this, we are willing to pay a higher price for diamonds than for ordinary pebbles. We guard them when they are in our possession, we show them off at special events, and we even insure them in case they are lost or stolen. But we ignore most other rocks and stones, using them only when necessary for landscaping or construction. We have chosen to value diamonds over other kinds of rocks, and this choice—this assignment of value—influences our actions.

The same is true for our relationships. What fear says is a rock to be cast aside, love sees as a diamond to be cared for and cherished. Appraising our relationships as highly valuable means that we are willing to pay a price for them. We choose to protect them when they're threatened or come under attack. We take actions that may not come naturally or easily to us and others might mock as foolish. However, when we recognize the value of our close personal connections, we make them our highest priorities.

> What fear says is a rock to be cast aside, love sees as a diamond to be cared for and cherished.

The fundamental way we care for our relationships is with regular investment of time and energy. Without our physical presence and emotional engagement, our relationships cannot be sustained for long. Left unchecked, a loved one's irritation transforms into exasperation and then anger, which eventually leads to alienation and estrangement. Fear tempts us to treat our relationships with apathy regarding such efforts because people are unpredictable and can cause us discomfort and pain. But the fearless family knows the risk is worth the investment. And so we take the time, make the effort, and choose people over things.

Even when heartbreak happens and difficulties *do* come, we still choose not to give up on others. If you get food poisoning from a restaurant, you don't give up on food. True, you will likely never eat at that restaurant again. You might never eat that specific food again. But within days you will eat again, and a week later you will likely be eating at other restaurants. In much the same way, we should learn from bad relationship experiences, and they shouldn't cause us to give up on connecting with others. Nor should they cause us to fall for the false promise that material things can replace people in our lives. They can't.

Him, Us, and Them

In the Home of the Brave, we place a high value on people and relationships. But that doesn't mean all relationships are of equal worth. Let's take a look at how we are meant to approach three different classifications of connection.

Him

In the Home of the Brave, everything begins with how we relate to God, for "unless the LORD builds the house, the builders labor in vain" (Psalm 127:1 NIV). In all things, He comes first. From our most mundane, everyday activities to our loftiest long-term goals and aspirations, we are to keep the Lord at the forefront of our thoughts and plans while giving Him preeminence in our hearts:

> Whether you eat or drink, or whatever you do, do
> all to the glory of God. (1 Corinthians 10:31)

Commit to the LORD whatever you do, and he will establish your plans. (Proverbs 16:3 NIV)

You shall love the Lord your God with all your heart and with all your soul and with all your mind. (Matthew 22:37)

Whereas most other religions are based on a system of rules and regulations designed to appease one or more gods and/or goddesses, Christianity is first and foremost about a relationship. People were created to live in close personal fellowship with God. The original fellowship was severed by Adam's sin, but Jesus has made fellowship with God possible once more, reconciling to God all those who believe and are washed clean by the blood Christ shed on the cross for our sins.

God wants us to know Him, not just know *about* Him. Through the sacrifice of Christ, He beckons us to enter into close, personal relationship with Him as His adopted sons and daughters (Romans 8:15). He wants us to draw near, remaining in His Word and talking and walking with Him every day. In this way, we will recognize His commands not as a buzzkill, but as a loving invitation to a better way of life, like a compassionate plea from a wise father who is trying to keep his children from harm.

God's sovereignty also extends to our earthly relationships. His plan is to use our relationships with one another to transform our hearts and cultivate love in our lives. But every relationship must be viewed through the lens of our relationship with Him.

Us

While we are commanded to love everyone (Matthew 22:39), we have a unique responsibility to those who are members of our household. Far too often, however, we neglect these relationships. Sometimes it's a problem of familiarity. The longer we're around someone, the easier it is to lose interest in everyday interactions with that person.

As we've seen, our biggest problem is not boredom but fear of intimacy. Whether or not the choice is a conscious one, we often distance ourselves from the people closest to us because they know our faults and failures better than anyone. That's why many people can be transparent with strangers online yet not be able to tell their spouses the whole truth of how they feel or what they think.

Familiarity makes us nervous, but the fearless family understands the value of being known. We honor all relationships, but we treasure our connections with the people under our roof.

Them

Although we prioritize our relationships with God and family, we don't ignore those outside of the home. We seek to connect with a diverse group of people. We take the lessons we are learning in the midst of committed love and extend that love to others. While those inside the home have unique perspectives because of how well they know us, those outside the home enrich us because they bring to a relationship backgrounds, experiences, and perspectives different from what we're accustomed to.

Relationships and Stress

When one of my children is experiencing heightened anxiety, my first thought as a parent is to do everything in my power to remove, or at least lessen, the stressors causing the anxiety. If the kids are nervous about an approaching thunderstorm, I will move them to the center of the house to muffle the sound of thunder and keep them from seeing the lightning. If they've been struggling to get to sleep at night because they're afraid, I try to make sure they don't watch any scary programs or commercials before they go to bed.

If something is causing our loved ones stress, a commonsense approach is to distance them from the source of anxiety. (This is a form of the flight option in a fight, flight, or freeze response.) While this approach may be helpful, it's rarely possible to shield a person from all points of stress. In fact, it can be debilitating long term if this is how we teach our kids to always deal with their fear. Many people have grown up learning to avoid issues rather than coping with circumstances that make them uncomfortable. Avoidance can be useful, but it's not the best approach to dealing with stress.

A second approach is often recommended to us but we rarely implement it. Stress can have a more profound effect on us when our emotional, physical, and spiritual energies are depleted. When we fail to rejuvenate by getting sleep, eating right, and exercising daily, we make it possible for anxieties to have greater control over us. How many times have you been deeply worried about a situation, but after a good night's rest you saw the circumstance in a new light and were relieved? Any time our stress is high, we must ask ourselves if our energies are low. A healthy meal, good sleep, and moderate exercise can help to keep anxiety from overwhelming us.

When stress is high, we all think about removing ourselves from the source of anxiety. Some of us consider how to strengthen our ability to endure stress. But there is a secret weapon that most of us never think to employ to combat stress and anxiety: our relationships. Strengthening our connections can greatly weaken the impact of worry.

Anxiety is both a cause and an effect of being disconnected. It's easy to see how stress can hinder our bonds with others. Fearing what others might think of our situation and lacking the courage to be vulnerable, we (consciously or subconsciously) push others away during seasons of high anxiety. What we often overlook, however, is that being disconnected isolates us from a potential source of strength—our family and friends.

Deep, meaningful bonds with others give us a sense of security, value, and control over our circumstances. When our connections are active and strong, so is our ability to endure stress. We instinctively know this to be true for children. If my child is worried about an approaching storm, I try to shield him from the sights and sounds of the storm. But if that doesn't work, I take him in my arms and hold him as tight as possible. This connection with me doesn't make the storm go away, but it empowers him to endure it. This is not something we grow out of. No matter our age, meaningful connection with others strengthens our ability to withstand stress. In fact, our level of anxiety often says more about our relationships than it does our circumstances.

So when our *children* are stressed, our first question as parents should be "How can we strengthen their bonds with us and others?" Rather than focusing on correcting our kids or trying to talk them out of their fears, we need to find ways to connect with them and make them feel loved and secure.

When *you and I* are feeling stressed, our first question should be "How can I strengthen my bonds with my spouse, family, and friends?" While it's fair to consider whether it's possible to lessen our stressful inputs and bolster our ability to endure pressure, the more significant weapon at our disposal is drawing strength from our relationships.

Making the Choice to Connect

We should value others to such an extent that our relationships influence our schedules, dictate our actions, and determine what must be done today and what can be put off until tomorrow. Too often, we push an opportunity for connection aside to accomplish what feels like a more demanding item on our to-do list. When we do this, we are setting ourselves up for a fall.

We need to recognize that while lunch with a friend or a phone call with a mentor might not produce immediate visible results, these precious moments of personal connection are much more important than the daily "emergencies" that fill our calendars. After all, everyone has a need to connect regularly with at least a few people. When we deny this need in ourselves and others, we suffer negative consequences.

Granted, few things in life are as complicated as relationships. The greatest sorrows in life almost always take place in the context of relationships—death of a loved one, divorce, heartbreak, and so on. Yet our greatest comforts also come through relationships—the soft touch of a grandmother, the healing kiss of a mother, the supportive hug of a spouse, the handshake of a friend. In the Home of the Brave, we acknowledge the risks but choose to connect anyway.

Think on These Things

1. What can we learn from observing the Trinity about what makes for a strong relationship?

2. Why are we tempted to choose a connection with things over a connection with other people? What can people provide us that things cannot?

3. Think of a past or present relationship in which you have held back a part of yourself from the other person. Why have you held back? What might happen in your relationships if you were fully engaged?

4. What steps can you take immediately to improve your relationship with God? How might growing closer to Him impact your relationships with the people in your life?

Chapter 10

Submission: Open Hands vs. Closed Fists

Do nothing from selfish ambition or conceit, but in humility count others more significant than yourselves. Let each of you look not only to his own interests, but also to the interests of others.

Philippians 2:3–4

Submit to one another out of reverence for Christ.

Ephesians 5:21 NIV

Tearing down the Home of the Afraid and building the Home of the Brave are difficult tasks, but they're not really counterintuitive. Most of us understand the importance of good relationships. We know that a healthy heart is essential to our well-being. Even trust, while we might struggle with it, is known to be a worthwhile pursuit. But the final wall of this new home goes against natural inclination. We hear the word *submission*, and we bristle. The word conjures images of violence, oppression, surrender, humiliation, degradation, and defeat.

When I was in high school, I coached youth baseball at the Boys Club. During my senior year, I coached a team of eleven- and twelve-year-olds. I was never a great player, which is why, as a high school student, I was coaching and not playing baseball. However, I did have one above-average ability—I could throw strikes. From my early days in Little League, I always had a place on the team because, whatever the situation, I could find the strike zone with my pitches. So one of my great joys as a coach was teaching young pitchers how to throw strikes.

During my final year of coaching, the kid who was our primary catcher wanted to learn how to pitch, so I began working with him after every practice. He developed quite quickly and soon began asking when he would get to pitch in a real game.

One night, right before game time, I was told the other team didn't have enough players to field an official team. They would have to forfeit, but they still wanted to scrimmage, so I loaned them my best player and we started an unofficial game. This was the perfect time to put my catcher on the mound and let him pitch. Unfortunately, I didn't think of doing that. I just stayed with the usual lineup, although I had the option to make changes during the game.

When the father of the catcher realized what was happening, he became irate. He stormed into the dugout and demanded to know why his son wasn't being given a chance to pitch. I realized then it was a great idea. However, I couldn't make a last-minute change at the behest of an angry parent, so I chose to stick with my lineup. The father grew even more upset and yanked his kid out of the dugout, calling me a few choice names as they walked off the field of the Goldtrap-Gardner Boys Club.

I look back on the situation with a sense of irony and sadness. The dad was right, but he was wrong. He was right that I should have thought to pitch his son, but he was wrong in how he handled it. This father blew a tremendous opportunity to show his son how to respect a coach (or any authority figure) even when the coach is wrong. He had the chance to teach his son to give a hundred percent effort even when things don't go your way. He could have shown his son how to wait for his time and then take advantage of the opportunity.

I have often wondered about that father and son. I wonder if, when the son got to high school a few years later, he rebelled against his father and if the father was livid that his son didn't respect him. The father would likely never realize that his son was doing just what his father had modeled for him.

Because of our natural, fear-driven need for power, our gut reaction to authority is usually to rebel. Nobody likes authority. We are so repulsed by the idea of being controlled by others that the very concept of submission is abhorrent to us. And when someone in power attempts to subjugate others against their will, it is evil. Generations of people have twisted the idea of biblical submission for their own purposes as a way to exercise control over others. This type of action must be rejected.

However, the concept of submission should not be dismissed. There is great beauty in people willingly submitting themselves to one another out of love and respect.

What Is Submission?

Submission is an idea so foreign to our nature that we often fail to understand what it is. Consider a yield sign. As I'm merging from an on-ramp onto a highway, a yield sign is sometimes present to remind me that if another car is already in the lane I'm headed for, I must allow the other driver the right-of-way and then fall in behind her. To submit in a relationship means that I'm yielding my will to another.

> Submission is an idea so foreign
> to our nature that we often fail
> to understand what it is.

The fact is, we submit in life far more than we realize. By remaining in the country we are in, we are choosing to submit to that country's rules and laws. When we accept a job to work for a company, we are agreeing to submit to the hierarchy of the organization. When we apply for a driver's license, we are consenting to operate our motor vehicle according to the rules of the road. Playing sports, signing contracts, buying tickets to a show, even striking up a friendship—all involve making a choice to submit to certain rules, conditions, and/or authorities.

We have been taught to fear that submission to human authority will lead to oppression, and submitting to the wrong people or institutions can do just that. Some of our greatest stories of courage and heroism are about those who were unwilling to submit to injustice. Yet submitting at the right times to the right people does not hold us back or lead to forced subjugation. Instead, it opens the door to freedom, simplicity, unity, empowerment, and joy. This happens as we let go of the need to control and forgo having everything our way in order to lovingly put the needs and desires of others ahead of our own.

Of course, submission in the home begins with submission to God. We submit to Him both as individuals and as a family. We obey, respect, and honor Him as the ultimate authority in our lives. We recognize that His ways are higher than our ways and that it is far wiser to follow His path than to insist on our own. We bend our wills to His. Submission to God leads to life. In Proverbs 3:1–2, He tells us, "My son, do not forget my teaching, but let your heart keep my commandments, for length of days and years of life and peace they will add to you."

Mutual Submission

The Home of the Brave is dependent on mutual submission; if this second wall is weak, it puts the entire home at risk. But submission is possible only after we have laid the foundation of trust and prepared the roof of heart. If two or more people are finding it difficult to submit to one another, chances are there's a lack of trust and/or weakness of character involved.

We can all agree that submission *feels* unsafe. And as long as we are still idolizing safety, we will never submit to anyone. Only when we let go of the constant pursuit of safety can we begin to consider submitting to God and others. Trust empowers our ability to submit. If we trust and see that God is good, powerful, and at work among us, we can begin to surrender our wills to His. But wait—this will happen only if we have also given up the idol of appearances. If we're busy trying to project a persona of strength, submission is a no-go. We must value heart and character over appearances before we can think about submitting to anyone.

Even if we can submit to God, we do so knowing that He is a higher power and authority and deserves to make the decisions. But it's more difficult to submit to others who are just as fallible as we are. Yet if we are motivated by love, if we are learning to trust one another, and if we are more focused on the heart than on appearances, we can find the freedom that comes with submitting to one another.

What does this look like at home? First, we must lovingly and willingly submit to each other in marriage (Ephesians 5:22, 25). High divorce rates are a symptom of husbands and wives being unwilling to submit to each other. When we say "I do," we agree to put the well-being of the marriage above our whims and selfish desires. Indeed, we are choosing to submit in ways that other people might find foolish. As a husband, I have vowed to give up certain freedoms in exchange for the fidelity and commitment of my wife. To many in this culture, this crazy notion sounds like the exact opposite of how to enjoy life fully. But anyone in a healthy marriage knows from experience this is the pathway to a fulfilling relationship. And despite what the world says, happy married relationships *are* possible.

When children enter the picture, we also submit to a new calling. I'm not talking about who's really in charge; the parents are in charge, but having children requires that we make the deliberate choice of setting aside certain hopes and dreams to raise healthy, loving, godly human beings. Parenting is demanding. It's costly. Yet it's worth it.

Sometimes I Submit to My Kids

Submitting to God also means there are times when I must submit to my children. While I have God-given authority over them, their mother and I are not the ultimate authorities in our home. God is. Because we all submit to Him, my children have the right and responsibility to hold me accountable to the rules we have set in place.

Admittedly, it can be uncomfortable to be a guest in our house. If we're eating dinner and my phone vibrates, I sometimes instinctively look to read a text I've received. If my daughter catches me, she calls me out. "No phones at the table, Daddy." Thinking this is a bit disrespectful, our guests nervously watch to see how I will respond to being publicly corrected by my child. On good days, I say, "You are right, Ella. Thank you for reminding me." I put my phone away, and the conversation continues. On bad days, I may not be as gracious in my response, but the result is the same—the phone goes back in my pocket as I submit to my daughter's correction.

Other times, it is my unique responsibility as a parent to enforce rules, though that should be the case as infrequently as possible. The line of authority in our home is clear: Jenny and I make the rules, and our children must submit to the rules. However, the more my children can see that we all must submit to rules, the more effective the rules will be. Instead of always thinking of me as the authority, they need to see me as someone who also must submit to others. It's valuable for my kids to witness me interacting and cooperating with God, police officers, sports officials, government leaders, etc.

One way we can communicate the importance of obedience to our children is by allowing them to hold us accountable. They have every right to call us out—in private or public—when we don't adhere to the truth as we have taught it to them. For example, my kids can hold me accountable to:

1. God's Word. In our house, the ultimate authority is God. Each of us is to submit to what God has said in the Bible. Therefore, my kids are allowed to call attention to anything I say or do that might contradict Scripture. The Bible tells me to love my children and discipline them, but it also instructs me not to exasperate or provoke them to anger (Ephesians 6:4). So they have every right to ask, "Dad, is this punishment loving?" I am called to submit to the Lord's instruction, and my kids can help me do so.

2. My word. While my word doesn't carry the authority of God's Word, my kids should expect me to do as I say. Therefore, they have the right to remind me of what I have said, both to them and in teaching others. It is not disrespectful for them to remind me of my word and to expect that I will not contradict myself. They also have the right to expect that I will keep my promises. On occasion, circumstances make it impossible, and when they do, my kids deserve an explanation from me.

3. House rules. Every home has rules. In healthy homes, the rules are spelled out and not just assumed. While age and maturity may dictate some exceptions (bedtimes, for example), most of the rules must be right for everyone. Many of the things my kids are not allowed to do are things I shouldn't do either. In these areas, my kids are allowed to hold me accountable to follow the same rules I expect *them* to obey. Because they are house rules, everyone is expected to obey them, and everyone has the authority to enforce them.

As my children hold me accountable in these three areas, it helps them better understand their own behavior and makes it more likely we all will obey.

Honoring dinnertime is one of our house rules. Although our schedules and responsibilities won't always let it happen, we work hard as a family to make sure all four of us (usually five because my mom joins us) eat together five or six days a week. One part of honoring dinnertime is not bringing things to the table that could distract us. My kids are not allowed to have electronics at the table, and neither am I. Just as I can remind them, they can remind me.

We Are Saved to Serve

We submit to God. We submit to authorities (Romans 13:1–7). We submit to the people who share our home. We submit to our brothers and sisters in the family of God (Ephesians 5:21). But we are also meant to submit to those in need, people who can do nothing for us in return. This is the ultimate reversal for a world built on the quest for power. People in a society that values strength seek to *be* served, or we serve in hopes that our actions will somehow be to our own benefit. But a home built on love thinks differently. We look for opportunities to serve those who can't possibly do anything for us in return (Luke 14:12–14) and, in so doing, serve God (Matthew 25:40–45).

To better understand this, let's return to the opening scenes of the greatest story ever told. In recounting the Christmas story, the gospel of Luke tells of not just one birth, but of two. In addition to the nativity of Jesus, Luke also goes into detail in portraying the birth of His cousin John the Baptist. John was born to older parents, Zechariah and Elizabeth, who had long been unable to conceive a child. In fact, John's birth is considered miraculous because Elizabeth was well past childbearing age.

For a man, few things bring perspective like the birth of a child. While a woman endures nine months of morning sickness, fetal kicks and stretches, and an expanding midsection as a constant physical reminder that she is a mother, a father's first real contact with the infant is seeing the child and holding him or her for the first time. It's a moment that cannot be described with mere words, and it can bring sudden clarity unlike any other experience.

When his son was born, Zechariah was filled with the Spirit and spoke a prophetic prayer of blessing that not only foreshadowed the child's remarkable future, but also told of something Jesus would bring to this world: "to grant us that we, being delivered from the hand of our enemies, might serve him without fear, in holiness and righteousness before him all our days" (Luke 1:73–75). Zechariah revealed that one of the great purposes of God's redemption story— from humanity's beginnings in the garden and now culminating in the life of the Messiah—is to free us so we may serve God. In other words, we have been saved to serve.

Of course, not everyone feels the need to be saved. Outside the church, without a belief in God or His standard of holiness, humanity fails to recognize its sinfulness and therefore sees no need for a Savior. But once we accept the truth about God and who He is, our sinful condition is made clear and it becomes relatively easy to accept

Jesus as being our only hope for redemption. *Inside* the church, we have a different problem. We may understand what Jesus is saving us *from*, but many of us don't know what He is saving us *to*. Yes, He saves us from sin, but He saves in order that we "might serve Him."

> Yes, Jesus saves us from sin, but He saves in order that we "might serve Him."

God does not save us so we may serve ourselves and our own interests. He does not save us so we may search for meaning and fulfillment in success, wealth, or possessions. He does not save us so we may call on Him like a genie in a lamp who will grant our every desire.

No, God saves us so we are able to do what we were created to do: serve Him. We are saved to serve.

More Than Occasionally

When we speak of serving God, we often think of momentary acts of worship such as praying before a meal or singing in church on a Sunday morning or going caroling during the Christmas season. While these are pleasant, and perhaps even important, Zechariah was speaking of something more. Much more.

Zechariah was a priest, and he and his wife "were both righteous before God, walking blamelessly in all the commandments and statutes of the Lord" (Luke 1:6). Everything he did was for God. His great longing was to be able to serve God better. But sin prevented him from being everything he wanted to be; it prevented him from serving God with all his heart. When Zechariah proclaimed that the Messiah would save His people to serve, he wasn't talking about ushering twice a month or even teaching Sunday school. He was talking about a whole life devoted to God. Zechariah said "all our days." It's not just about Sunday. It's not just about special occasions. Every day and in every way, salvation frees us to serve God.

God created us to serve Him, and none of us can find our true purpose or inner peace until we are doing what we were created to do. This might not mean a dramatic change in *what* we do, but it does mean a significant shift in *why* and *how* we do it.

Consider a stay-at-home mom with two small kids. Her day consists of nursing a baby, chasing a toddler, managing the home, running errands, planning and preparing meals, caring for her husband, and much more. Then God delivers her from the grip of sin. What changes in her day-to-day life? Probably not much. Her newfound salvation doesn't mean that her baby stops crying, her toddler slows down, her marriage gets easier, and her life becomes a breeze. Very little of *what* she does changes. But she has been freed to serve God, which means *why* she does what she does changes dramatically.

No longer is she raising her kids to please herself or give them a good life; she is now charged with making Jesus known to them. No longer is her marriage all about her or her husband; it is now a vehicle through which she may know Jesus and make Him known. *How* she does a lot of things probably changes too as she learns from the example of Jesus and understands how He calls her to live life.

Consider a high school student. He goes to school, plays in the marching band, and enjoys hanging with his friends and playing video games. Then God delivers him from the grip of sin. What changes in his daily life? Maybe a few things. Maybe he adds some prayer time and Bible study, but primarily his life continues as is. Salvation doesn't mean he can skip school or is free to disobey his parents. *What* he does probably doesn't change, but *why* and *how* he does it will certainly change.

As he's looking at colleges and considering a potential major, he now looks to Jesus and tries to emulate Him. Maybe he chooses to go into the medical field to help people. Perhaps he will study engineering with an eye to build homes in the missions field. Whatever he decides, it will be based on a desire to make Jesus known and make this world a better place. Having been delivered from the shackles of sin, this high school student is now free to use all of his gifts and talents not on himself, but to bring glory to God.

Giving God Glory through Submission

Some Christians seem to think they have been saved for the sole purpose of getting into heaven when they die. They act as if God has very little to do with everyday life; He simply offers a better life after this one. Others believe that their salvation requires that they attend church on Sundays, put a few dollars in the plate each week, and contribute to the annual bake sale, but otherwise, God makes no demands on the rest of their lives. Many of us believe that daily life is mostly secular and has little to do with God. But these are all unbiblical views of salvation.

You and I were created to serve God, but sin prevented us from doing so. Salvation restores the created order and makes it possible again for us to serve Him. Zechariah saw that the Messiah would save us for the purpose of serving God. He knew that our service is not limited to a few acts each week. Zechariah saw life in a holistic sense, recognizing that everything we do has the potential for bringing glory to God.

We serve God at home by serving and submitting to one another. Families, while never perfect, can be places where we grow in love and the knowledge of the Lord as we learn and practice what He has taught.

We serve God in the marketplace by living what we preach, working with integrity, serving and submitting to our employers and colleagues, and putting in our best effort every day. Occupations are more than jobs. They are callings in which we do what we do to make this world better and bring glory to God.

We serve God in our churches by doing more than talk about what is wrong with the world; we also take action to make it better. We serve and submit to our brothers and sisters out of reverence for Christ. We love and encourage and support each other. We examine God's Word together and teach the truth, while also holding one another accountable to the truth.

That's the story of Jesus. His whole life led to the cross, but His life wasn't only about the cross. His birth brought glory to God, causing others to worship and marvel at God's goodness and mercy. As a boy, He learned His father's carpentry trade and amazed teachers in the temple with His understanding of God's Word, and He grew "in wisdom and in stature and in favor with God and man" (Luke 2:46–52). His ministry and teaching brought glory to God. His healings and miracles brought glory to God. His friendships brought glory to God.

Jesus submitted to the Scriptures that they would be fulfilled, even when they prophesied His humiliation and death. On the night before

His crucifixion, He asked that the cup of suffering be removed from Him but nevertheless submitted to His Father's will (Matthew 26:39).

As it was for Jesus, so it is to be for us. At every stage in life, in every aspect of life, God wants to deliver us so we may serve Him. And we serve Him, in part, as Jesus did—by serving others (Mark 10:45; Galatians 5:13).

Whereas the world would have us serve ourselves and grab all that we can, when we choose to forgo our own desires and submit our schedules and resources for the sake of others, we are proclaiming a different way of life—a better way of life. By choosing to serve as Jesus served, we are turning people away from a life of fear and pointing them toward a life defined by love.

Think on These Things

1. What are some ways you submit to God individually and as a family? What are some areas in which you need to take decisive steps to submit fully to God?

2. What are some of your house rules? If they aren't written down, make a list of seven rules that guide your house, then share them with the family. (Example: No phones at the dinner table.)

3. How did Jesus model submission for us in a way that shows its beauty? List some examples.

4. What are some ways you can follow Christ's example by serving and submitting to the people you interact with every day?

Chapter 11

Courage: What Every Day Demands

Have I not commanded you? Be strong and courageous.
Do not be frightened, and do not be dismayed, for the
LORD your God is with you wherever you go.

Joshua 1:9

When I am afraid, I put my trust in you. In God, whose word I
praise, in God I trust; I shall not be afraid. What can flesh do to me?

Psalm 56:3–4

When we moved into our current home, our kids were young, just three and one. While the neighborhood was great, several of the homes around us had garage apartments that were rented out to different people every few months. We wanted our children to enjoy the large backyard, but with a steady stream of strangers overlooking our property, we felt the need to provide a bit of security for the kids. So we got Ruby.

Few things are as cute as a German shepherd puppy, with those big, attentive ears. But as these dogs quickly grow into handsome adults, they develop a new trait—the ability to terrify people. Although Ruby is really loving and energetic, to a stranger she is all muscle and teeth and very intimidating. Ruby has one job: protect the children. Where they go, she goes. I'm convinced that she would bust through a window to protect my kids.

Ruby is a ferocious dog—most of the time. But she does have one flaw: Ruby is terrified of cats. The dog who scares everyone and everything cannot handle the sight of a feline. If a cat comes anywhere near, our intimidating guard dog barks, runs, and hides. Her fear transforms her. Ruby steps outside of what she was created to be and becomes something radically different.

Fear has a similar effect on people. We were created to be so much more than we are. Fear was never meant to define us, and yet these days, no word better describes our state of mind, individually or collectively. In fact, fear has become so commonplace in our lives that we don't even recognize its presence in most situations. We act out of fear without even realizing it.

> Fear was never meant to define us, and yet these days, no word better describes our state of mind.

We know something's wrong, but we're not always sure what it is. We only know that we're uneasy, uncomfortable, and vaguely unhappy with our lives and our circumstances. And so we look for ways to control the situation without really understanding the problem. That's why we give so much time and energy to securing our safety, projecting appearances, collecting material possessions, and leveraging power—things that further add to our anxiety. As our fears grow, they can take a terrible toll on us as individuals, families, and communities.

Still, we share platitudes on social media about the virtues of trust, character, connection, and service, but we know these things sound too good to be true. We have a hard time believing they work in the real world. We think the way of love is only true in fairy tales—and then for someone else, not for us. That's because in life, as in fairy tales, the way of love takes something we often don't have: courage.

What Is Courage?

Courage is an attitude that leads to action. It's having the strength of character to face danger, endure hardship, or risk injury in order to do the right thing. In terms of physical courage, think of the Allied soldiers storming the beaches of Normandy on D-Day, or Sergeant York single-handedly attacking and defeating an enemy machine-gun nest that had pinned down his fellow soldiers in World War I. In terms of moral courage, a good example from fiction is Atticus Finch, the lawyer who stands up against his racist white community to defend a black man, Tom Robinson, falsely accused of rape.[1]

What does courage look like in a family?

A young man and woman solemnly vow to love, honor, and cherish each other until death despite not knowing what the future holds.

A family member wisely shows verbal restraint in response to another's harsh words said in anger.

A young person humbly seeks help from a sibling to deal with a problem that can't be overcome alone.

Family members treat one another with respect and common decency while enduring difficult times together.

Hard words are spoken in love, but not in a harsh way.

One's personal sins are confronted for the sake of both the individual and the family.

A family member seeks—and receives—forgiveness.

Unfortunately, courage is not the default choice in most of these situations. Instead, cowardice is the norm. Cowardice is a refusal to do the right thing because of the immediate possibility of discomfort, suffering, or risk of injury or rejection. It's second nature for us to deal with a problem by running, hiding, denying, or lying to avoid further discomfort. However, our natural response is rarely the right response.

Building the Home of the Brave often requires that we do what does *not* come naturally: choose pain or discomfort in the short term to experience health and victory in the long term.

When Courage Is a Must

Courage is needed in every aspect of a relationship, but there are five specific areas where courage is demanded:

Courage to Face the Truth

A relationship is real and durable to the extent that it deals with the truth. A marriage might appear healthy, but it's not a genuine relationship if denial and falsehood persist between husband and wife. When parents and children refuse to admit what both know to be true, their relationship is a facade. Intimacy demands honesty. Only when people openly show their true selves to one another can they experience meaningful love.

Courage to Run toward One Another and Not Away

If the first temptation is to hide from a problem, the second temptation is to run from it. It takes boldness for us to turn *toward* each other in those moments when we want to bolt and run. It's only when we come together that we can do the work necessary to move the relationship forward. When families continually turn away from one another, they create an atmosphere of distrust where mutual support is lacking and broken relationships are the rule.

Courage to Reject Ungodly Values

Society very clearly values money, possessions, and power. Without the courage to choose a different path, we will value the same things the world around us values. We must tenaciously develop and hold to a different set of priorities in which we honor relationships, pursue authenticity, allow ourselves to be vulnerable, and willingly serve one another, even when ridiculed by a society that rejects those things. Our choices might even be met with skepticism by those we love, but we must reject the worldly values of others without dismissing them as individuals created in God's image.

Courage to Forgive and Seek Forgiveness

Nothing feels riskier than asking for forgiveness, unless it's forgiving someone who has hurt us. In a survival-of-the-fittest culture, it makes little sense to admit our own faults or to refuse to utilize the offenses of others against them. Our social instincts tell us we must hide our weaknesses and exploit the vulnerabilities of others to our advantage. It takes courage to reject our natural inclinations. But to ask for, and freely give, forgiveness is necessary for building healthy relationships.

Courage to Endure

Cowardice is quick to give up. It's an attitude that assumes failure, avoids pain, and changes direction at the first sign of danger. This is a terrible way to approach a marriage. Courage expects hardship, embraces discomfort when it comes, and has a dogged determination to endure. A healthy marriage requires both spouses to choose to do whatever it takes to grow and mature that relationship. This means more than simply deciding not to divorce. Choosing health is a higher call. But for that choice to become a reality, both husband and wife must have the courage to endure.

The Fruit of Courage

How can you know when your home is making healthy strides in these areas? Courage produces three primary fruits in any relationship. When families continually make the courageous choices instead of the cowardly ones in their interactions, they will develop these three visible characteristics as a family: growth, maturity, and connection.

Growth. Courageous relationships produce a persistent pattern of growth. Because family members endure the temporary pain that conflict creates, they can learn from each instance and make changes.

For a family with grit, conflict becomes something of a gift because it is often the source of growth. When a relationship gets stuck and fails to grow, it's usually a sign that courage is lacking in one or more aspects of the relationship.

Maturity. Cowardice is caused by immaturity, and it enables immaturity as well. Courage, on the other hand, matures us. It allows us to move past and leave behind childish behaviors, immature actions, and adolescent mindsets. A family of mature individuals is often the sign of a courageous family.

Connection. Courage draws people together. When a husband and wife boldly walk through life together, trusting and being open and honest with each other, they create a deep and lasting bond. They might experience more moments of disconnect, but they will reap the rewards of their courageous choices. As parents and children learn to communicate well and their relationship changes, they will find that a meaningful connection is one of their greatest strengths. Contrarily, in many cases, a lack of connection is a sign of cowardice.

Who Will Step Up and Go First?

Consider: Does your family consistently demonstrate courage in communicating with one another and resolving conflicts? What about your relationships outside the home? Are they marked by courage or cowardice? Healthy relationships of any kind demand courage. Few people in unhealthy relationships understand the role of cowardice in their brokenness, and recognizing its influence is an important step toward combating it.

Every week, I deal with broken relationships—marriages on the brink of divorce, lifelong friendships that are deeply frayed, bosses exasperated by their workers, employees dismayed by their employers, citizens and community leaders appalled at one another. While each of these situations contains unique elements, rarely am I confronted with a problem that's unusual. Sometimes, someone just needs an outsider's fresh perspective or a small piece of new information, and they are on their way. But far more often, the parties in a fractured relationship don't require more information. In most cases, they already know what needs to happen; they simply lack the courage to do it.

"I'll go first" are three words that can transform any relationship. When we know the right and proper action necessary to mend a relationship, we must have the courage to take the first step.

> ## "I'll go first" are three words that can transform any relationship.

Now it's true that in many aspects of relating to others, we should rarely go first. Too many family and work interactions are hindered by the selfishness of one or more parties. In most situations, we should be the last to be seated, be served, speak, become angry, draw conclusions, make assumptions, pass judgment, and so on.

But when conflict arises, we need to be the first to do the right thing. We need the courage to act and lead. Healing often begins after one person takes the initiative to do what needs to be done. As Billy Graham said, "Courage is contagious. When a brave man takes a stand, the spines of others are often stiffened."[2]

Let's look at some times when you need to go first:

Be the first to break the silence. When you have had a falling-out with someone, it's tempting to run, avoid, and remain silent. It's less stressful to talk *about* people than to talk *to* them. But it's more productive to break the silence and seek reconciliation. If you're in a relationship that's broken, be the first one to make a call, send a text, speak, or take any action that opens the door to reestablishing the relationship.

Be the first to admit fault. Denial is easier. It's more comforting to downplay your mistakes and to blame others. But taking responsibility for your actions and admitting wrongdoing makes for a powerful statement and announces to others that they are safe with you to admit their own mistakes. Being the first to admit fault creates the possibility for tremendous change. But as long as you're living in denial, everything will stay the same.

Be the first to change. When relationships go wrong, environments become toxic. Families grow cold, workplaces become uncomfortable, and communities become vengeful. While it's easy to point fingers and list all the ways others need to change their actions and attitudes, it's not as easy to look at yourself. Model the behavior you want to see from other people. If something needs to change, let the change begin with you.

Be the first to forgive. One of my favorite worship songs begins, "Everyone needs compassion." We all need forgiveness, and because our need is so great, we should be quick to forgive others (Mark 11:25). This doesn't mean you must ignore offenses or downplay disputes. It does mean you should refuse to hold others' mistakes over their heads.

Be the first to act. Words are easy; actions are not. The habit of humanity is to drift toward apathy and inaction when faced with a need. If you want to be different, take action. If a situation needs work, be the first to step up. Others might criticize you for acting hastily, but those are just critics being critics. While they are busy talking, you will be busy leading.

"I'll go first" are three of the most powerful words in the English language. They can be as impactful on a relationship as "I love you" or "I forgive you." If no one will step up and say these words, families will remain estranged, businesses will remain ineffective, and communities will remain split and disengaged. But when someone displays the courage to go first, it creates a climate in which others must choose whether they will respond in kind. Taking the first step doesn't guarantee change, but it does create an environment in which change can take place.

Turn Around and Take the Narrow Path

One of my great privileges as a pastor involves walking alongside people during their most difficult days. When an affair comes to light, a painful diagnosis is delivered, an arrest is made, or someone just reaches his or her breaking point, many people call their pastor. As we sit in my office or their living room, I can see clearly that a family, a relationship, or a life hangs in the balance. On too many occasions, I have sat there certain that life as they know it has ended, that whatever blow has been experienced is fatal.

What surprises and delights me, however, is how often this isn't the case. I regularly sit with people who are experiencing unimaginable pain, but it's not a pain that will tear their family apart or break up their relationship. Instead, their crisis will be the turning point that leads them to experience joy, health, and connection they never imagined possible.

What is it that makes the difference? Courage. Some couples have the tenacity to continue showing up and fighting for their marriage. Some parents and children refuse to quit working toward a better relationship. Some families keep fighting for one another and are willing to work however long it takes to break through the obstacles they face.

Those who overcome these situations are not smarter than other families. It's not as though they have a special gift or anointing that others lack. In most cases, it is that they choose the way of courage even when dealing with heartbreak, loss, or deep sorrow. These people are willing to lean in to their pain in hopes of discovering emotional healing. Individuals are ready and willing to be vulnerable even though they have every right to be skeptical about the commitment of the other person(s).

When I talk with couples or families on the brink of destruction, I understand that they have a perspective that's different from mine. As they sit there, all they can see is pain. They are burdened with a sense of hopelessness. They have walked the same path for such a long time that any suggestion of change seems overwhelming, if not impossible.

But I see something different. While their circumstances may seem unique to them, they're often quite commonplace from where I'm sitting. Many times the names and details have changed, but the problems are the same issues I heard about last week, last year, and last decade from families like theirs. And because some time has passed in previous cases, I know the outcomes. In almost every situation, I can think of individuals or families in similar circumstances who not only survived their crisis but are in a better place than ever before.

When meeting with people in times of trouble, I often plead with them to have the courage to walk the path toward healing. I remind them what Jesus said about the wide and narrow gates (Matthew 7:13–14). There's an easy way to go through life, and there's a harder way. Most people choose the easy way, the one that requires very little of them. This is the safe road, the low-risk, low-reward path. On this road no one has to make an effort to get to know the heart of another or to be made vulnerable by revealing anything of themselves beyond the most superficial appearances. This road is wide enough and smooth enough to take along all the possessions and power they cling to for comfort. It's the easy, less painful route, but it's the way that leads to death, and it will kill their hopes, their dreams, their families, and their futures.

But there is another way. It is the narrow path that few dare to travel. It is the hard road of humility and maybe humiliation. This is the high-risk, high-reward path. To walk this road, people often have to submit, to lay bare their souls to another—a counselor, a pastor, a trusted friend, a loved one. They have to be willing to endure pain to get where they want to go. I often compare it to climbing up on the operating table and allowing God to perform open-heart surgery on them without any anesthetic. In fact, that is precisely what I'm requesting they do. While I understand their fear and trepidation, I ask them to trust me because I know many people who sat in the same place where they're sitting and chose the narrow way—the way that leads to life. They did the work, they allowed God to operate on their hearts, and their lives were eternally changed.

The difference between the Home of the Afraid and the Home of the Brave comes down to the courage to choose the narrow, harder way. It doesn't take grit or bravery to go with the flow and head in the same direction as everyone else. It's not difficult to opt for safety, appearances, materialism, and power, when everyone around us is chasing after those things and encouraging us to want them too.

The courageous choice is to make an immediate U-turn and go against the flow. Yes, it will feel unnatural to trust when you want to hide, connect when you want to run, serve when you want to rule, or forgo instant gratification to go after a bigger prize that requires trust, patience, risk, and work. But this is the way of Jesus, and it's the way of life and love. The road is harder and the way narrower, but it's marked by deeper satisfaction and lasting rewards. And the destination is much greater and far more wonderful than you can imagine.

When You're Afraid, Choose Love

We can't expect to completely eliminate fear from our lives. The Home of the Brave is not devoid of anxiety. Fear is a human emotion and is often a realistic first response to bad news, impending loss, and the harshness of living in a fallen world. But just because we feel fear does not mean we have to be ruled by it. We can feel afraid and then make the conscious decision to choose the way of love. That's what it means to be a fearless family.

In the Home of the Brave, we know that when fear comes knocking, we will be tempted to take refuge in those things the world says are valuable. We recognize the temptations and then reject them. We choose instead to go the way of love—to trust even when it feels risky, to reveal our hearts instead of putting up a front, to work through our problems with loved ones instead of buying more stuff, and to submit willingly instead of insisting on doing things our way.

We're not always going to get it right. It's too easy to slip back into old patterns of thinking and former habits. Yet even when we fail, we deal with our failures differently. Instead of denying our mistakes, we recognize our faults, confess our failures, and immediately change direction.

The choice to love is not a one-time-only decision. It's a daily process in which we must reject fear, spurn temptation, and choose to put the needs and desires of family, friends, colleagues, and neighbors ahead of our own. Sometimes we are confronted with this choice moment by moment until we slam the door on fear and cut ourselves off from the source of temptation. It's not always an easy decision, but it is a simple one.

While the application of love might be complicated now and then, the basic thrust of what we are to do is always the same. Love. In every circumstance, no matter who is involved, we are to choose the loving action.

Of course, love can be demanding. Discerning what the most loving choice is can be time-consuming and difficult. When arguing with your spouse, stop and determine the loving way to approach each other. Rather than allowing fear to provoke you to raise your voice or emotionally shut down, work out how you can lovingly discuss the issue at hand and together make the most loving choice.

Facing a problem you don't know how to handle? Choose love. Admit the problem, work together, and seek an expert's opinion if necessary. Be transparent about the issues. Be willing to change your mind or adjust your attitude if that could help with the solution. Do the best you can, but be prepared to change directions if you recognize that you're going the wrong way. Be patient with each other and quick to give grace.

Remember that fear will likely be your fallback position, and decide beforehand not to go there. Learn your weak spots. When are you most likely to be ruled by fear? What are the bad habits you can fall into if you aren't paying attention? Recognize your fear, then refuse to let it drive your decision-making. Maybe you can't kick fear out of the car, but you don't have to let it drive. Put it in the passenger seat or stuff it in the trunk, and you make the conscious choice to be driven by love.

Think on These Things

1. Review the five areas in which courage is demanded of us. Which of these have you had trouble with in the past? How is this tendency affecting your current relationships? What do you need to start doing differently?

2. Consider the three fruits of courage—growth, maturity, and connection. Based on the descriptions of these characteristics and their presence in your home, how would you rate your household in terms of courage? What about your friendships or your workplace?

3. Think of an issue in your home (or at work or among friends) where someone needs to go first to begin the healing. What action needs to be taken? Will you take the necessary first step?

4. Are you in a relationship that stands at a crossroads, a stalemate, or a turning point? What could be achieved if both of you were willing to do the hard work necessary to break through the obstacles between you?

Tomorrow's Family

*I sought the LORD, and he answered me and
delivered me from all my fears.*

Psalm 34:4

"Dad, I'm anxious."

Had I heard these words three years ago, I wouldn't have known what to do. It would have been tempting to blow them off, to downplay my son's childish fears in order to focus on the "real" concerns of adult life. Maybe I would have panicked out of fear that my child was facing an insurmountable challenge we couldn't handle together.

But after the past few years of walking with Silas through his struggles and recognizing the role that fear has played in my own life, these were good words to hear. Saying "I'm anxious" is a great sign of health. He recognized his fears, communicated them, and sought help with them. It was a sign of how far we had come.

"Oh, really?" I responded. "What are the tools you are going to use to work through that?"

Silas listed the things he could do—focus on his breathing, think through the positive things he would experience the next day, visualize his past successes, talk with me about specific things that might be causing him nervousness.

It's been three years since we first became aware of our son's anxiety. Since then, we have been on a path of discovery to learn what triggers his fears and what tools are most effective for navigating his worries. But the journey hasn't only been about Silas. In seeking help for him, Jenny and I have discovered the role fear plays not just in our family but in every family.

What we learned has opened our eyes. While we felt love for each other, we weren't always successful in living out that love. Too often, fear was driving our communication and our choices. And when fear drives, we rarely like the destination.

Today we're doing a better job of not just feeling love for each other but actually loving each other. We are by no means perfect. Nearly every day we uncover another area where fear is expressing itself, or we find ourselves drifting back into old patterns of idolizing safety or overvaluing appearances. But we now have a framework through which we can diagnose new problems and create reasonable solutions together.

As we enter into the next stage of parenting—teenagers!—we do so with a little less fear and a lot more hope. We know that sometimes we will feel fear, but love will drive our decisions. Safety will be a consideration, but trust will be our foundation. We won't spend much time concerned with appearances because we'll be too busy guarding our hearts and raising kids of character. When we are bored or angry and are tempted to find comfort in things, we will instead make the effort to connect with each other. When we're tempted to throw our weight around and exert control over a situation, we will instead choose mutual submission, knowing that serving each other is more likely to lead to the outcome we desire.

Tomorrow, I will meet with a family to discuss the funeral for their patriarch. It's a meeting I have once or twice a month. The less I knew the person in life, the more important these meetings are. I'll bring out a blank legal pad, then ask the family questions while jotting down key words and stories that defined this person's life. Inevitably, I will get a sense of the home in which the person created and the kids were raised.

A day is going to come when I won't be sitting at that table. Instead, my family will gather with a guy like me, and he will be asking them questions about who I was and what defined me. My hope is when that time comes, the generations who come after me will use words like *trust, integrity, relationship, service, courage,* and *love* to define our lives together. I want them to be able to say, "Dad experienced anxiety, but he didn't let it control him. He was nervous by nature, but he always chose the way of love." I want them to talk about how faith and love defined our family in good times and bad. I want them to laugh about the times we had and cry at my departure. But even in their grief, I want them to know how to move forward because I modeled for them how to navigate tough times.

Whether you recognize it or not, every day you are choosing to be led by something. Chances are it's fear or love. With every decision, you are placing another brick on your home, another tile on your roof. We live in a world overwhelmed by fear. Have the courage to choose to build the Home of the Brave.

Notes

Chapter 1: Fear Is a Bad Driver

1. Timothy Keller, *Counterfeit Gods: The Empty Promises of Money, Sex, and Power, and the Only Hope That Matters* (New York: Dutton, 2009), xxiii–xxiv.

2. Elisabeth Kübler-Ross and David Kessler, *Life Lessons: Two Experts on Death and Dying Teach Us about the Mysteries of Life and Living* (New York: Scribner, 2000), 138.

Chapter 2: Safety: The Wrong Question I Regularly Ask

1. *John Mulaney: New in Town*, Netflix (2012).

2. Barry Glassner, *The Culture of Fear: Why Americans Are Afraid of the Wrong Things* (New York: Basic Books, 1999), xxi.

3. Benoit Denizet-Lewis, "Why Are More American Teenagers Than Ever Suffering from Severe Anxiety?," *New York Times Magazine*, October 11, 2017.

4. John Gramlich, "Five Facts about Crime in the U.S.," Pew Research Center, October 17, 2019, www.pewresearch.org/fact-tank/2019/10/17/facts-about-crime-in-the-u-s.

5. Christopher Ingraham, "There's Never Been a Safer Time to Be a Kid in America," *Washington Post*, April 14, 2015, www.washingtonpost.com/news/wonk/wp/2015/04/14/theres-never-been-a-safer-time-to-be-a-kid-in-america/.

6. Tim Elmore, *Generation Z Unfiltered: Facing Nine Hidden Challenges of the Most Anxious Population* (Atlanta: Poet Gardner, 2019), 84.

7. Ingraham, "There's Never Been a Safer Time."

Chapter 3: Appearances: A Bad Umbrella

1. Henry Wadsworth Longfellow, "The Rainy Day," *Ballads and Other Poems* (1842).

2. Syreeta McFadden, "Rachel Dolezal's Definition of 'Transracial' Isn't Just Wrong, It's Destructive," *Guardian*, June 16, 2015, www.theguardian.com /commentisfree/2015/jun/16/transracial-definition-destructive-rachel-dolezal -spokane-naacp.

3. "Dave Ramsey's Act Your Wage! Board Game," DaveRamsey.com, accessed August 11, 2020, www.daveramsey.com/store/product/dave-ramseys-act-your -wage-game.

4. Matthew Frankel, "The 100 Best Warren Buffett Quotes," Motley Fool, August 30, 2019, www.fool.com/investing/best-warren-buffett-quotes.aspx.

Chapter 4: Materialism: To Have More Is to Fear More

1. "The Dow's Biggest Single-Day Gains and Losses in History," Fox Business, March 17, 2020, www.foxbusiness.com/markets/the-dows-biggest-single-day-drops-in-history. In the relatively early days of the COVID-19 crisis, the Dow Jones plummeted 2,352.60 points on March 12, 2020, but regained 1,985 points the next day.

2. Adam P. Brownlee, "Warren Buffett: Be Fearful When Others Are Greedy," Investopedia, April 5, 2019, www.investopedia.com/articles/investing/012116 /warren-buffett-be-fearful-when-others-are-greedy.asp.

3. Peter Brown and Robert Rans composed the music and lyrics for "Material Girl." The famous music video takes its key imagery from Marilyn Monroe's iconic performance of "Diamonds Are a Girl's Best Friend" in the 1953 movie musical *Gentlemen Prefer Blondes*. In the video, Madonna plays an actress singing on a soundstage, surrounded by tuxedoed male dancers offering her various jewel-encrusted baubles in return for her affections. Few today remember that the song-and-dance sequences are interspersed with scenes suggesting that, contrary to the lyrics, Madonna's actress likes the simple things and is more impressed by daisies than diamonds.

4. Brian Regan, *I Walked on the Moon*, directed by John Brenkus, DVD (Irvine, CA: Conversation Company, 2004).

5. Robert Beard, "Covet," Dr. Goodword's Office, accessed August 11, 2020, www.alphadictionary.com/goodword/word/covet.

6. The tenth commandment is, however, uniquely related to the first, "You shall have no other gods before me" (Exodus 20:3). When we covet the possessions of others, we eventually end up worshipping those objects, or others like them. When we violate the tenth commandment, we have already broken the first.

7. Thomas J. Stanley and William D. Danko, *The Millionaire Next Door: The Surprising Secrets of America's Wealthy* (Lanhan, MD: Taylor Trade, 1996).

8. Avi Dan, "What Do You Call a 17-Year-Old Ad Campaign? Priceless," *Forbes*, August 25, 2014, www.forbes.com/sites/avidan/2014/08/25/what-do-you-call -a-17-year-old-ad-campaign-priceless/#279d019f7142.

Chapter 5: Power: The Path to Paranoia

1. Kevin A. Thompson, *Happily: 8 Commitments of Couples Who Laugh, Love, and Last* (Grand Rapids, MI: Revell, 2018).

Chapter 6: Love: The Antidote to Fear

1. Dietrich Bonhoeffer, *Life Together* (New York: Harper & Row, 1954), 97.

Chapter 8: Heart: Above All Else

1. C. S. Lewis, *Mere Christianity* (New York: Harper One, 2001), 47.

Chapter 9: Relationship: Choosing People Over Things

1. On March 11, 2020, the World Health Organization announced that it was classifying the COVID-19 outbreak as a pandemic. But it wasn't until later that evening, when Tom Hanks announced that he and his wife, Rita Wilson, had tested positive for the coronavirus, that the reality of the situation hit home for many of us.

Chapter 11: Courage: What Every Day Demands

1. In a 2003 poll, the American Film Institute named Atticus Finch the greatest movie hero of all time over the likes of Indiana Jones and James Bond. Gregory Peck played Atticus in the 1962 screen adaptation of Harper Lee's novel *To Kill a Mockingbird*.

2. Billy Graham, "A Time for Moral Courage," *Reader's Digest*, July 1964.